Minneinneopa

150 Year History
Minneopa State Park

by Gordon H. Herbst

For more informaton, write to:

Gordon H. Herbst
20499 555 Lane
Mankato, MN 56001

Book design by Scott W. Roemhildt
Publishing by Akorn Creations, LLC, 677 390th Ave., Janesville, MN 56048

ISBN: 978-0-9790885-1-3
Printed in the United States of America by Quality Print, Waseca, MN

Cover photo of Minneopa Fall taken in 1887. W.B. Smith is standing at the right of the
upper Falls. (Blue Earth County Historical Society Photo)

TABLE OF CONTENTS

Minneinneopa

The recorded history of the area can be traced back almost 350 years.

Many accounts of Minnesota history first record Groselliers and Radisson to the area in 1659. Shortly thereafter, the Jesuit missionaries arrived in this area.

It was in 1700 that LeSueur ascended the Minnesota River and established Fort Huillier at the junction of the Blue Earth and LeSueur Rivers. This is the best written record we have of explorers and traders in our area. The fort they built at this junction was abandoned in 1702 because of adverse Indian activities.

Other fur traders have been reported in the area, but written records of their activities have not been found.

Additional activity in the Minnesota River Valley included an Indian mission established at Traverse des Sioux in June of 1843. Also the first frame house built in the Minnesota River Valley above Fort Snelling, was by Mr. Pond, who had the lumber brought up from Point Douglas at this time.

It was 1849 when the steamboat "Anthony Wayne" ascended the Minnesota River to near Traverse des Sioux. A week later, the steamboat "Yankee" ascended beyond the Blue Earth River.

The Traverse des Sioux Treaty was signed in 1851 and settlers began rolling into the new land, settling close to the river valley.

The year 1858 brought statehood status for Minnesota. Now it was part of the United States of America.

The next decades brought difficult times for the settlers. The Civil War was raging (1861), Indian attacks were taking place (1862), and a grasshopper invasion in 1873 lasted for five full seasons.

That same year, 1873, ushered in other excit-

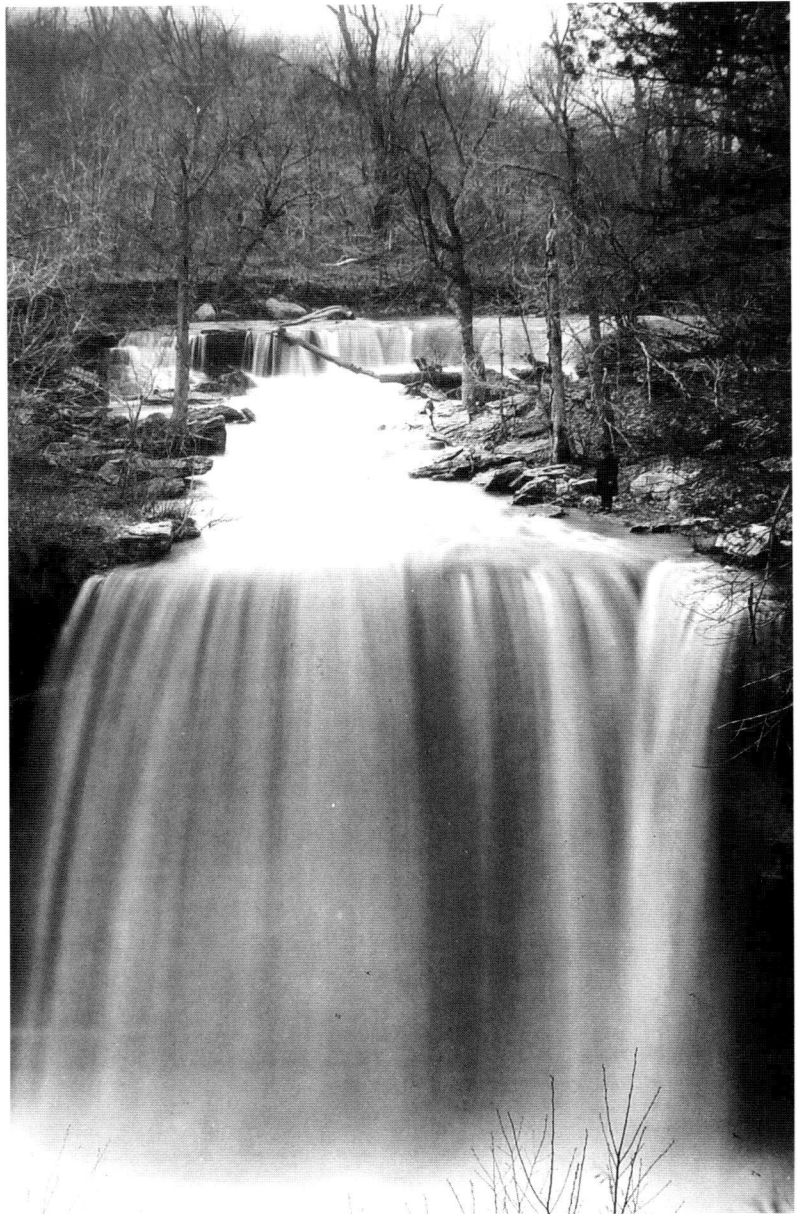

Minneopa Falls in 1887 - W.B. Smith is standing at the right of the upper Falls (*Blue Earth Co. Hist. Soc. Photo*)

ing times on the frontier. A visit by the outlaw James-Younger Gang to the Northfield Bank gave law officials, settlers and the early newapapers something to talk about (TV would have had a field day!).

Most of the history attached to the area comes from the Native Americans. Winnebago, Dakota and Sioux Indians were native to the area. The inquisitive may even find old settlers who will tell them of Indian braves, who in their frail canoes boldly rode over both Falls, landing at the bottom right side up!

The *Mankato Weekly Review*, April 11, 1882, describes Minneinneopa Creek (water of two falls), as "coming from basins of Crystal and Lily Lakes, coming together and going their way along the winding course to the turbid Minnesota River."

The spelling and translation of Minneinneopa has had many variations. George Clark (MFP 11/24/1905) states the meaning by the Sioux Indians was "water of the dancing elk," not "water of two falls," in 1851 and 1855. Later the name was abbreviated to Minneopa. Minneopa Creek also had several names, including Schwatzer Creek and Lyons Creek.

The *Review* went on to say, "but the Falls claims the greatest attention, as no more beautiful and picturesque spot can be found in Blue Earth County. Yet the citizens of Mankato and adjoining communities fail to see that making a summer resort at Minneinneopa Falls would directly benefit these communities. It would attract strangers, who would see this for the first time and be so attracted that they would want to make their home here."

The Railroad Depot no longer has a place near the tracks but still can be identified. It was used for the Park office until a new one was built recently. The many train passengers are a thing of the past. The depot used to be located close to the track, where the train would board and discharge passengers who wanted to stop at the Falls.

From the station you could hear the murmur of the Falls. During the spring runoff or after a heavy rain, the thundering of the Falls was near deafening.

As the temperature lowered below freezing, the Falls would begin to freeze. If water was plentiful, a solid cone of ice would form measuring 55 feet high and 25 feet in diameter at the base.

Mr. J.B. Hodge was the railroad depot agent and was very proud of the waterfalls. It is said that the walls of the station were decorated completely with pictures of the Falls area. The creek was just a few steps from the depot and often Mr. Hodge would accompany the visitors over to the Falls.

It is through his efforts that this natural summer resort became so widely known. He convinced the railroad company to have a special rate to and from Minneopa during the summer and advertise the attractive features of this place. There were trains leaving Mankato at 7:55 a.m., 10:45 a.m., 12:15 p.m. and 8 p.m. The fare was 20 cents.

In 1903, a real effort was made to bring people to visit the Falls. It was estimated that 13,000 people made the trip to the Falls that year. People from Mankato, Lake Crystal, Madelia, Vernon Center, Good Thunder and Mapleton would come to the Falls, often for a picnic.

"The growing business capacity of Mankato would indicate Minneinneopa must keep pace, for it is the only convenient resort for the tired hands and heads in this part of the state. It is in Mankato's interest to see that they do not throw away a beautiful gem, such as the Falls."

An earlier book entitled, *"History of Minneopa State Park,"* by Thomas Hughes was published in 1932. It is written in Hughes style and I would encourage people to read it.

The first Minneopa Railroad Depot. The white painted sign reads: Minneopa Falls State Park. ca. 1870s (*Blue Earth Co. Hist. Soc. Photo*)

Minneinneopa Falls.

These beautiful Falls are situated about five miles from Mankato, and is one of the most picturesque cataracts in the State. It is already one of the most popular places of summer resort for picnic parties and pleasure seekers in the surrounding country. The beautiful Natural Scenery surrounding it is unsurpassed. The main fall is about 65 feet perpendicular. All that is needed to make it one of the most important stopping places on the St. Paul and Sioux City Railroad, for pleasure parties and health seekers, is the erection of a Good Public House for their accommodation and entertainment.

Its manufacturing advantages only need improving to become valuable. It is the outlet of the cluster of lakes known as Mills, Loon, Lilly and Crystal, and the supply of water can be regulated at the outlet.

The proprietor now proposes to convert the forest surrounding it into a HANDSOME PARK, and persons visiting the Falls are requested not to tie their Horses to the trees between the Railroad and the Falls.

Any one desiring to invest in what can but be a profitable investment—building a nice house for the accommodation of pleasure seekers, would do well to call on the proprietor at his residence.

SOUTH BEND, August 13th, 1869.

D. C. EVANS.

CHRISTENSEN BROTHERS

DEALERS IN

DRY GOODS, GROCERIES,

Yankee Notions, Hats and Caps,

CROCKERY AND GLASSWARE,

(*Corner of Front and Jackson Streets,*)

MANKATO, - - - MINNESOTA.

AGENTS FOR THE

Solicitation in the *Mankato Record - Weekly*
August 14, 1869

Minneinneopa Park Hotel

Miner Porter came to Mankato from Fox Lake, WI, in 1857 and pre-empted a tract of land near South Bend. He started to build on this property in 1858, which became known as Minneinneopa Park Hotel.

It was built on his farm located just east of the Falls and one half mile west of South Bend. The local sawmills had black walnut and butternut lumber for inside finishing which he purchased. The pine lumber which he used for the framing of the building was hauled from St. Paul by ox teams, which took all summer.

The hotel served people visiting the area for health, pleasure and business reasons. The short distance from Minneopa Creek made it a headquarters for visitors to the Falls. It was a popular place for travelers and permanent boarders who were looking to buy and sell land. It was a stopping place for people traveling towards Winnebago and Blue Earth City.

Pigeon Hill was a mile west of the hotel and was used by the Sioux Indians as a camping grounds during the winter of 1858. They were supposed to stay on their reservation at Fort Ridgely, but were constantly coming and going in the area. The Winnebago Indians also roved at will over the entire country. All of the settlers considered the Sioux Indians a blood thirsty lot and when the alarm was spread, Mrs. Porter would take the children to the old stone mill in South Bend where they would spend the night.

Mr. Porter later fitted the grounds as a summer resort for visitors with a picket fence, arbors, gates, shrubs, plants and vines which were brought into Minnesota from nurseries. The pleasant groves surrounding his premises, and arbors with vines promoted the pleasure of visitors. It was stated that a resort like this had long been needed and the newspaper editor hoped that the people of Blue Earth County

Minneinneopa Park Hotel - *ca. 1861 (Blue Earth Co. Hist. Soc. Photo)*

would reward Mr. Porter with patronage commensurate with his enterprise.

He had a thriving business until the Sioux Uprising in the early 1860's which discouraged many travelers from coming to this area.

At about this same time, there were invasions of locusts (grasshoppers) which ate nearly everything green. Crops were devoured and the settlers had little food to survive the winter. Hard times were taking a severe toll on the area. Visitors did not return to the hotel seeking pleasure as before. By 1870, the hotel visitors were so few, that the hotel was closed to pleasure seekers.

The first Blue Earth County Fair was held at the hotel on Oct. 11, 1859. It was well attended and it lasted all day and into the dark hours.

The building was struck by lightning in 1866. Mrs. Porter was thrown to the floor and stunned. The chimney was shattered. A fire was started on the roof but the heavy rain extinguished it.

Later, Blue Earth County made arrangements with Mr. Porter to care for the county charges and the former hotel was used as the "county home" for several years.

About 1898, W.W.P. McConnell and Mrs. Defransa A. Swan, a teacher in the Normal School, became the owners of the farm and operated the first bottle milk dairy using the milk from Jersey cows raised on this farm with great success.

The residence on the Minneopa Dairy Farm, formerly Minneinneopa Park Hotel, was destroyed by fire in February 1906, from an unknown cause. The first floor was occupied by two families and the upper floor was used for storage.

The farm, sometimes referred to as the Minneopa Farm, was now owned by Mrs. D.A. Swann.

A new house was built for the dairy manager and it continued in operation for several more years. In 1935, several of the old barns and foundations were still in use and visible.

A Local Place of Resort.

Minneopa Falls, one of the most romantic and beautiful spots in our State, and the charms of which are hardly outlined by the above picture, should be owned and held by Mankato interests. As the country grows in population and wealth, all such places will become valuable, and by taking hold of the matter now and securing it, it may be developed and beautified. The distance from Mankato is only five miles, less than an hour's drive, or may be reached at almost any hour of the day by trains on the Omaha road.

Our attention is called to this matter by the possibility of its passing into other hands, where it may not be used as a public resort or its natural beauty preserved.

If fifteen or twenty of our young, active business men would combine and purchase this property, which they can at a price which bears no relation to its actual value, then lay out the adjacent land in village lots, upon which to build pleasant little cottages, it soon may be made one of the most desirable resorts in the State, and a source of profit to the sagacity of the men who thus take hold of it. We cannot recall a better opportunity in the whole State, and it is a matter of surprise that it has lain so long in its present condition.

A Local Place of Resort
Mankato Review, July 1, 1884

South Bend and Minneopa

D.C. Evans was the first person to have ownership of the Minneopa Falls. He states that when he came to South Bend in 1853, he found a log shanty 4-5 logs high at the Minneopa Falls. He and Tom Lamaraux estimated the logs had been there 15 years. They heard a Mr. Schwatzer had built the structure. The creek at that time was called Schwatzer Creek.

It is reported by the old timers of the area, that David Taylor of LeCrescent had visited Minneopa Falls in 1853, 1856 and 1871.

Shortly after Captain Humbertson left for St. Paul in 1853, Isaac S. (I.S.) Lyons moved to the settlement of South Bend with his family on July 31, 1853. Isaac was called "Buckskin Lyons" because he dressed in buckskin clothing.

The Lyons family came from Iowa in a covered wagon drawn by oxen with a cow tied behind. The family consisted of I.S., his wife, three sons and a daughter.

They bought a share in the South Bend townsite but withdrew it within a short time. The same year, they built in the glen where the old Sisseton Village stood. That was just east of the bridge which crosses Minneopa Creek on the Mankato–New Ulm road in Section 16.

The Lyons' were the first to build in the glen. They built a small log house at the foot of the hill, on the west side of Minneopa Creek, where present day State Highway 68 now crosses the stream on the Seppman farm.

Construction of the culverts and the highway have obliterated part of the old Lyons cabin site as well as the Indian Village site.

A short time later, the Lyons' family built a frame house on the same spot as the log house. Harvey Olson built the stone foundation for the frame house.

I.S. Lyons built a sawmill, which was the first mill on Minneopa Creek (sometimes called Lyon's Creek). The mill was located a few rods up the creek from his house. It started operation on August 8, 1854, but only operated for a short time.

A second saw mill was built near the mouth of the Minneopa Creek in the early 1860's by Owen Edwards.

John Lyons died on Sept. 9, 1854, while living in the glen and was the first white death in the settlement of South Bend. John was the son of Mr. and Mrs. I. S. Lyons. His burial services were held outdoors on September 11, 1854, at the D.C. Evans farm near Minneopa Falls. Burial was about ¼ mile west of the old cemetery boundary. He was 21 years old.

In later years, Minneopa Park was developed by the efforts of men from South Bend.

Top: **South Bend stone building**
Bottom: **South Bend townsite**
(Blue Earth Co. Hist. Soc. Photos)

The James-Younger Gang in Mankato

It was Sept. 7, 1876, when an attack on a bank in Northfield resulted in some unexpected events by all involved.

Two members of the bandit's party were killed during the attempted robbery. A bank cashier and Northfield citizen were also killed. The fighting did not stop with the withdrawal of the bandits. Posses followed the remaining six bandits for more than two weeks.

The escape route took them southwest of Northfield toward Mankato. The bandits were identified as Cole, James and Bob Younger, Jesse and Frank James and Charlie Pitts (alias George Wells).

During the next 14 days, these men were constantly pursued by posses and vigilantes. They suffered from cold, wet weather, poor shelter and what little food they could buy or steal from farmers. Hundreds of men were searching for them, so there was no real rest or recuperation. Their clothes were tattered from the brush and briars. Their wounds from the raid had no medical attention. They sometimes had horses to ride, but often walked to avoid capture.

Continuing in a southwesterly direction, the group approached Mankato and its numerous rivers. The bridges across the Minnesota and Blue Earth Rivers were guarded 24 hours a day, making crossing on the bridges a very high risk. The James' brothers left their companions near Mankato and rejoined them beyond the city, so they would not be so conspicuous.

The bandits were discovered near Mankato by a young man looking for his cattle. The men discussed how to dispose of the young man, but finally let him walk away. He promised not to tell who he had encountered, but alerted the law as soon as possible. This put hundreds of men out searching for the outlaws since there was a sizeable reward for the capture of the gang.

The county bridge over the Blue Earth River was well guarded, but the railroad bridge was guarded by two men and a boy. On Sept. 14, 1876, the trio were startled by rocks thrown into the nearby bushes. They decided not to investigate and the gang crossed the bridge, disappearing into the woods on the other side.

The *Mankato Record* reported that after the gang members had crossed the the bridge, they continued up the railroad tracks and stopped to eat in Gen. Mathews' melon patch.

When they reached the road up Pigeon Hill, they went into the woods about four rods from the track, and built a fire to prepare breakfast. The robbers fixed stakes in the ground and stretched blankets between them so they could not be seen from the tracks.

A man saw their camp near Minneopa Park and reported it. Another report came from a train engineer that someone was camped near Minneopa. A posse was sent to Minneopa to search for the bandits. They were stopped by a sentry who gave the alarm, alerting the gang. They made flight up Pigeon Hill and followed the woods to the Blue Earth River.

Following the surprise at Minneopa, the gang came out of the timber on the north side of Rush Lake. The James brothers got a horse from a nearby farmer and split from the rest of the gang. The James' rode south between the lakes, not knowing a picket line had been set up from Lake Crystal to the Blue Earth River. A guard shot at the brothers near Loon Lake, throwing them off the horse. The horse ran home and the James' fled into Mrs. Roonies corn field. Soon they found two gray horses on a neighbors farm and rode away, eventually going to Sioux City.

The Younger group heard the shooting at Loon Lake and returned to the Minneopa Creek area. They went undercover for 3-4 days before going west toward Madelia. They claimed to be hunters and got food from local farmers. They were recognized moving to Linden Lakes and eventually surrendered near Madelia.

After the robbers were captured, they were taken to Faribault and appeared before Judge Lord. There were reports that the prisoners would escape or be rescued, but those reports were termed hysteria designed to excite mob violence. After all, Minnesota is a law abiding state and these gangsters would be punished to the full extent of the law.

"The Gang" at Minneopa Creek Trestle

These recollections were reported to the *Mankato Free Press* on October 20, 1932, by John Riley of Lake Crystal. They were based on the search for the James-Younger Gang, which robbed the Northfield Bank on Sept. 7, 1876.

"When the gang came to Minnesota, over $100,000 in reward money was being offered by the express companies, bankers and railroad companies. Following the 'bank job' in Northfield, the robbers came to Mankato and on to Minneopa Falls. They stayed there for several days nursing their injuries.

Passengers riding the train spotted men camped under the trestle. They had their area covered with blankets to prevent being seen. Passengers reported to the sheriff these observations, which he investigated.

One morning while they were preparing breakfast, a train with detectives and sheriffs from Lake Crystal, 14 or 15, went down to about a mile west of Minneopa and walked close to the Park, while a second party of men from Mankato came toward the Park from the East.

The robbers were alarmed as they were getting their breakfast and left their camp. They fled into the timber to the south and came out of the timber near Rush Lake.

There was a small amount of gunfire exchanged. The James Brothers continued west to Sioux City.

The Younger brothers and Pitts heard the gunfire and turned back towards Minneopa Creek and went under cover for four days, claiming they were hunters when they stopped at settlers homes, asking for food. They wandered to the Madelia area where they were eventually apprehended."

Railroad trestle built over Minneopa Creek, which provided cover for members of the James-Younger Gang in 1876 *(Blue Earth Co. Hist. Soc. Photo)*

A Summer in the Big Woods

The author of this boyhood reminiscence is John Walker Powell, Jr. Powell was the son of pioneers who migrated westward from Indiana in 1855.

The senior Powell was identified with the Methodist-Episcopal Church for more than 40 years. He preached in many pulpits in western and central Minnesota, constantly moving his family from one frontier community to another. Shortly after arriving in the Minnesota Territory, the family acquired a farm on the Blue Earth River, a few miles southwest of Mankato in the Spring Island locale. The family retained the property for many years and would return to it on occasion.

John Walker Powell, Jr. was born in 1872 and was educated at Hamline University, the University of Minnesota and the Boston University School of Theology. He resided in southeast Minneapolis until his death in 1953.

He writes a story of a happy summer of his boyhood, starting in April 1882. It had been decided that John should go with his mother to the farm at Spring Island in the Big Woods country near Mankato where they would meet his big brother.

They arrived in Mankato, obtained a wagon and started for the country. They crossed the Blue Earth River on the new iron bridge (built in 1882) and proceeded through the virgin forest with budding trees, to the top of the hill where their little unpainted farmhouse stood on the hill at the head of a ravine. The garden was around the house and the fields were beyond. Mason Hynson's house was across the ravine.

After a week or more of cleaning the house and yard, it was time to plant the garden and flower beds. After the chores were done, their whole life revolved around the Blue Earth River. Fishing was an enjoyable sport.

The annual camp meeting of the Methodist Church in the Mankato district was held at Minneopa Falls. Near the head of the Falls stood a fine grove of young hardwood timber in a natural amphitheater which seemed to be an ideal place to have a camp meeting. The circuit riders and the people from farms and villages, some traveled nearly 30 miles, came and camped in a huge half-circle about the grove.

A speaker stand was built of rough pine boards at the foot of the slope, in the center of the surrounding tents. At the back of the stand was a shack known as the "preachers tent" with bunks for the visiting ministers. Plank benches to seat several hundred people were constructed in front of the stand and abundant clean straw filled the space about the altar, where the mourners knelt and prayed. A big tent served for prayer meetings and was used on rainy days.

Mrs. Powell purchased a bolt of unbleached cotton sheeting to make a tent and fly. A cookstove was set up under the trees at the back of the tent and a rough table was built of pine boards.

Sleeping arrangements were of the simplest; straw ticks laid on the ground were covered with abundant quilts. Kerosene lamps were hung in brackets on trees from both sides of the stand and the campers used lanterns and sometimes candles.

The beauty of the June woods and the excitement of cooking and eating under the trees was something to remember. The joy of sleeping in a tent, the smell of the canvas, the patter of the dew on the roof and the riotous mating songs of the birds thrilled many of the hearts at the meeting.

On camp-meeting Sunday, the people of neighboring Mankato turned out in full force, while the country folks came for miles. By 10 o'clock the grounds were filled with people, and the buggies and farm wagons were parked in ranks on the outskirts of the grove.

After religious services were done, the farmers retired to their wagons, the city people to their carriages and all would spread their picnic lunches on the grass.

The evening was filled with prayer and songs until midnight. This went on for six days. Then the tents were taken down, the preacher stand torn down and the lumber returned to the dealer from whom it was hired.

View of Spring Island (G. Herbst Photo)

Methodist Church Meeting at Minneopa
Date unknown - (Blue Earth Co. Hist. Soc. Photo)

Above: **Lizzie Jones at Minneopa Falls**
Below: **Ed Jones standing beside Minneopa Creek**
Both photos taken in 1902 (Blue Earth Co. Hist. Soc.)

Minneopa Park is Created

Negotiating the purchase of Minneopa State Park on Oct. 13, 1905

This photo was taken on the platform of the Minneopa Depot by J.P. Hodge, the depot agent. Seated *(left to right)* E.T. Young, State Attorney General; Samuel Iverson, State Auditor; John A. Johnson, Governor of Minnesota; General James H. Baker; Orange Little; and John C. Wise, editor of the *Mankato Review*. Standing behind them *(left to right)* Thomas Hughes, local committee member; F.G. Cuttle, Railway Construction Co.; Robert L. Williams *(in front of Cuttle)*; William W. Paddock, Chairman of the Blue Earth County Commissioners; Dr. J.W. Andrews, local committee member; Joseph R. Reynolds, *Mankato Free Press*; William L. Johnson, Superintendent of Railway Construction Company of Winston Brothers; and Chas. N. Andrews, local committee member. *(Blue Earth Co. Hist. Soc. Photo)*

PLEASED WITH PARK

State Officials View the Grounds Yesterday Afternoon.

They Were Delighted With the Magnificent Scenery.

Deal For the Pretty Site Will Be Concluded.

Was Fine Outing For the Governor and His Aids.

Governor John A. Johnson saw Minneopa park in all its splendor yesterday afternoon. So did Attorney General E. T. Young and State Auditor Iverson. These three state officials were delighted with what will soon be the commonwealth's new possession. They were not slow to express their approval of the action of the legislature in making provision for the purchase of this justly famous beauty spot. With one accord the gentlemen said that it was a wise move, and future generations will bless the men who had the foresight to preserve such an enchanting place. The rude spirit of commercialism will not be permitted to invade Minneopa. Its loveliness will always remain as it now is, and children yet to be will enjoy its grandeur.

Yesterday was an ideal day for a visit to the park. Under the bright Indian summer's sun overcoats were not necessary. The air was balmy, yet clear and refreshing. It was really a holiday for the state officials and they were more than pleased with the few hours they spent communing with Nature, and getting far away from the maddening throng. Governor Johnson was like a boy unfettered and released from school duties. He could walk about at ease and with no expectation of some hungry

Above: Map of Minneopa State Park, 1914
Left: Clipping from *Mankato Free Press*, Oct. 14, 1905
Below: The *Mankato Daily Review* reprinted an article from the *Minneapolis Tribune* which lauded the beauty of Minneopa State Park and its Falls. *Monday, Aug. 17, 1914*

MINNEOPA PARK LATEST BEAUTY SPOT IN STATE

Blue Earth County Has the Newest Attraction for Sightseers and Nature Lovers

Picturesque Falls and Shaded Lakes and Steams Lure Vacationists

Sunday's Minneapolis Tribune contains a splendid write-up of Minneopa state Park and Falls, near Mankato illustrated with several views, which will be of interest to our readers. The article follows:

when it built a station close to the park.

Soon after the park was made state property it was put in charge of W. R. Williams, an old resident, and he continued superintendent until his death on Dec. 24, 1913. Following his burial in a cemetery at the side of the park, his son, C. R. Williams, was made superintendent of the park. It was under his supervision that the new pavilion and other improvements were installed.

Minneopa is one of the most easily accessible of the state's parks, a railroad station of the Omaha line being but a stone's throw from the falls. The village of South Bend is near at hand, and Mankato is but five miles away, whence travelers from any direction may easily reach the park.

COL. C. H. SAULPAUGH IN AUTO ACCIDENT

Car Went Over Culvert in Ditch But No One Injured

On Friday last while Col. C. H. Saulpaugh, accompanied by Mrs. Saulpaugh, R. W. Foster and Fred Hawkins, was driving his Mitchell auto from Madison Lake to Lake Jef-

Above: **Enjoying the Falls** *ca. 1915 Below:* **Minneopa Creek near the upper Falls**. Note the Chicago, St. Paul, Minneapolis and Omaha train car on the track. *(Bl. Earth Co. Hist. Soc. Photos)*

RAPIDS MINNEOPA
PHOTO BY M&K.

Above: **Park visitors enjoy ice cream and drink at the refreshment stand.** *July 30, 1911.*
Below: **Minneopa Creek with Highway 169 bridge** *(Bl. Earth Co. Hist. Soc. Photos)*

Minneopa lower Falls and creek with wooden bridge *1916*
(Bl. Earth Co. Hist. Soc. Photo)

Minneopa Falls, Minn. State Park, Mankato.

Above: **Minneopa Park was the home to many ballgames.** *(left to right)* unidentified, unidentified, Robert Othoudt, Mr. Crane, Albert Othoudt, (man behind A. Othoudt unidentified), Bob Williams, unidentified, Walter Seppman and William Seppman *ca. 1915* *(Dorothy Paulson Photo)*

Below: **Minneopa Falls with rustic bridge** *1908* *(Phyllis Fall Photo)*

Culvert where the railroad crosses Minneopa Creek near the Falls.
(Bl. Earth Co. Hist. Soc. Photo)

This steam locomotive was on display by Earl Grice on the east edge of Minneopa State Park in the early 1970s. Every Sunday, Grice blew the whistle of this old relic.
(G. Herbst Photo)

Looking west along the railroad track in 2004.
(G. Herbst Photo)

George M. Palmer - 1942
G. Palmer was the contact person between the
local administration of Minneopa Park and State
Administration after the site became a State Park
(G. Herbst Photo)

GEORGE M. PALMER
1853 - 1939

AS A MEMBER OF THE LOCAL
ADVISORY BOARD OF MINNEOPA
STATE PARK FOR MANY YEARS,
MR. PALMER, IN OCTOBER 1927
INSTIGATED THE PLANTING OF
THE PLOT OF BLACK WALNUT
TREES NORTH OF THE RAILROAD
PLACED BY FRIENDS

George M. Palmer - Walnut Grove Commemoration
May 17, 1942 (Bl. Earth Co. Hist. Soc. Photo)

**Former Homestead
of
Robert & Frieda Ulmen
1950 - 1995**

Robert was park superintendent from 1936 - 1939 at Minneopa
State Park. He supervised the Works Progress Act (WPA) projects
and planted many trees that still thrive today. Frieda operated a
concession stand in the park that is now a visitor center.

Robert & Frieda's dream was to have the Ulmen Homestead included in
the boundaries of the park. After Robert's death in 1995, the land was
sold to the park so the public could also enjoy its beauty.

Dedicated by their Children
&
Minneopa State Park

2000

**Plaque recognizing
Robert & Frieda Ulmen homestead**
(Tim Pulis Photo)

The Louis Swanson farm, located east of Judson, now part of Minneopa State Park
1986 (G. Herbst Photo)

2005 Minnesota State Park Permit commemorating the 100th anniversary of Minneopa State Park.
(Minneopa State Park Photo)

JUN 06　JUL 06　AUG 06

MAY 06　　　　　　　SEP 06

APR 06　　　　　　　OCT 06

MAR 06　　　　　　　NOV 06

FEB 06　JAN 06　DEC 06

Minneopa State Park

Minneopa State Park Entrance
2004 (G. Herbst Photo)

Minneopa Creek, Falls and Canyon Geology

The Minneopa Park geology covers probably more than 5,000,000,000 years of time. The oldest units of sedimentary bedrock began forming before vertebrate animals.

The next layer, (younger in age) is a sedimentary rock. A third unit exposed is an iron cemented pebble conglomerate. It formed at the time the dinosaurs roamed the earth.

The climate grew colder over the next 80 million years.

Glaciers began advancing and retreating. The last glaciation began retreating about 12,000 years ago. The advancing and retreating of the glaciers left the landscape with unsorted clay, silt, sand, boulders and outwash streams and glacial lakes.

As the continental ice sheet retreated, the water was unable to flow north to Hudson Bay due to ice in the north.

The impounded ice melt water collected in Glacial Lake Agassiz. This is the largest glacial lake known - approximately 700 miles long and 200 miles wide.

Eventually the melt water overflowed to form Glacial River Warren. The repeated outpourings flowed down the present day Minnesota River Valley.

Lower Minneopa Falls spring thaw - kitchen in background
ca. 1920s (Blue Earth Co. Hist. Soc. Photo)

The Glacial River Warren has reworked the landforms we see today. The terrace levels represent the elevation of the river valley at the time. Examples of the large river valley are bedrock terraces strewn with boulders, sandstone cliffs, sand and gravel.

Minneopa Creek became a tributary to the Minnesota River over the last approximately 10,000 years. Headwater erosion caused the Falls to move upstream. Earlier the Falls was likely at the confluence of the Creek and Minnesota River. Given enough time, the Falls may erode to Lake Crystal. At some point, the Creek began flowing and encountered resistant layers (ledges of durable, well cemented sandstone). This durable layer has not eroded as quickly and formed a step-like staircase.

The softer sandstone below the durable layer erodes away relatively quickly, resulting in large pieces of sandstone at the bottom of the Falls.
(continued on page 33)

(continued on page 33)

High water over the lower Falls
1960 (G. Herbst Photo)

Above: **Rocks from the erosion of the Falls** *2006 (Jack Madsen Photo)*
Below: **Collapsed rock** *2006 (Tim Madsen Photo)*

Coal and oil in Minneopa?

The Minneopa area was explored for coal and oil by a locally formed company in 1886.

The area to be examined was about 600 acres from above the Falls to the Blue Earth River.

The Mankato Coal, Oil and Mineral Company organized in 1887 to prospect Minneopa Falls.

There is no evidence to suggest that any of those efforts were successful.

Reports of good fishing in Minneopa Creek

Reports of Minneopa Creek yielding 16 beautiful fish to one fisherman in three hours sounded like a good fish story.

A couple days later, the fisherman and a friend (witness) went fishing again in the Minneopa Creek and came to the newspaper office with a catch of 37 fine pickerel which they displayed and distributed to the neighbors.

Minneopa upper Falls
2006 (Tim Madsen Photo)

Right: **Minneopa lower Falls, frozen** *(Tim Pulis Photo)*

Below: **Minneopa upper Falls** *2000 (Tim Pulis Photo)*

Ice melt *2003 (G. Herbst Photos)*

Minneopa Creek filled with boulders
2004
(G. Herbst Photos)

Right: **Minneopa upper and lower Falls**
(Tim Pulis Photo)

Below: **Minneopa Creek wild water**
(Tim Pulis Photo)

DANGER

The Minnesota River Valley is a channel formed approximately 11,700 years ago. The view across the remnant of the channel is about one and one-half miles and about 200 feet deep.

At Minneopa Park, the river is much more crooked, which may be caused by the underlying bedrock. As the ice covered the area, a thick layer of glacial sediment and bedrock formed flat surfaces with steep slopes. The terraces in Minneopa State Park are erosional remants of the Ice Age flows.

The large boulders in the north part of the Park are typical granite boulders transported from Canada and Minnesota. Other rocks consist of gneiss, a banded metamorphic rock.

Geology and Landforms in the Park

Observations:

1. Confluence of the Minnesota River and Minneopa Creek
2. Minneopa Creek Gorge
3. Sandstone Cliff overlook
4. Waterfalls and sandstone amphitheater
5. Minnesota River flood plain
6. Overlook of the Minnesota River Valley from Seppman Mill
7. Walking the trail over the alluvial fan, east of Seppman Mill

Reference: *Surficial Geology of Minneopa State Park, Lisa M. Pottenger, July 1999, Minnesota Department of Natural Resources, Division of Lands and Minerals*

Rock ledge with eroding sandstone below it
2003 (G. Herbst Photo)

Canyon wall below the lower Falls
1999 (G. Herbst Photo)

Prominent columns of sandstone rock below the lower Falls
2000 (G. Herbst Photo)

Above: **Erosion, natural and man caused** *(Minneopa State Park Photo)*
Below: **Do you recognize any of your handiwork?** *(Minneopa State Park Photo)*

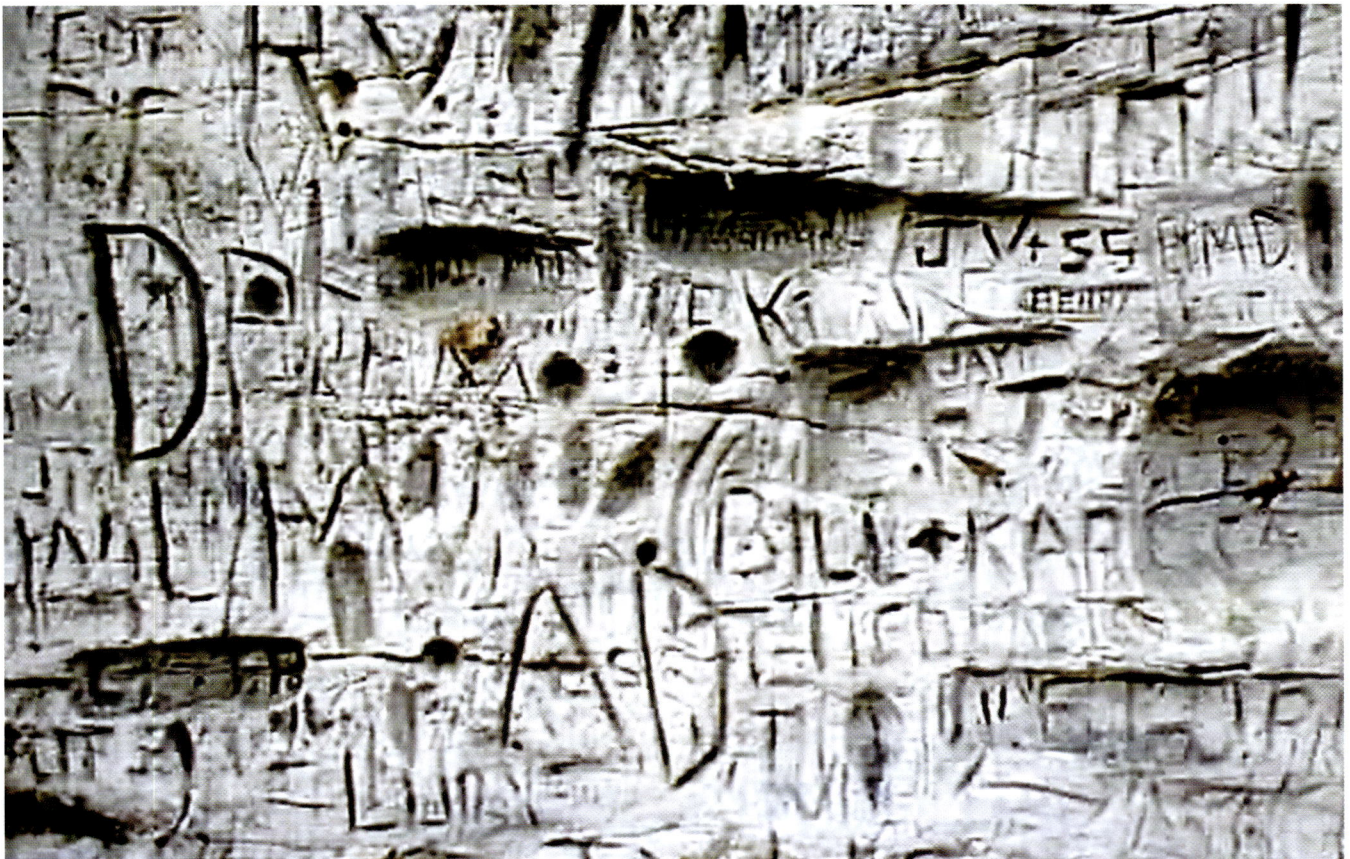

Above: **Upper Minneopa Falls** *2006* *(Tim Madsen Photo)*
Below: **Geology of the area well exposed** *2006* *(Jack Madsen Photo)*

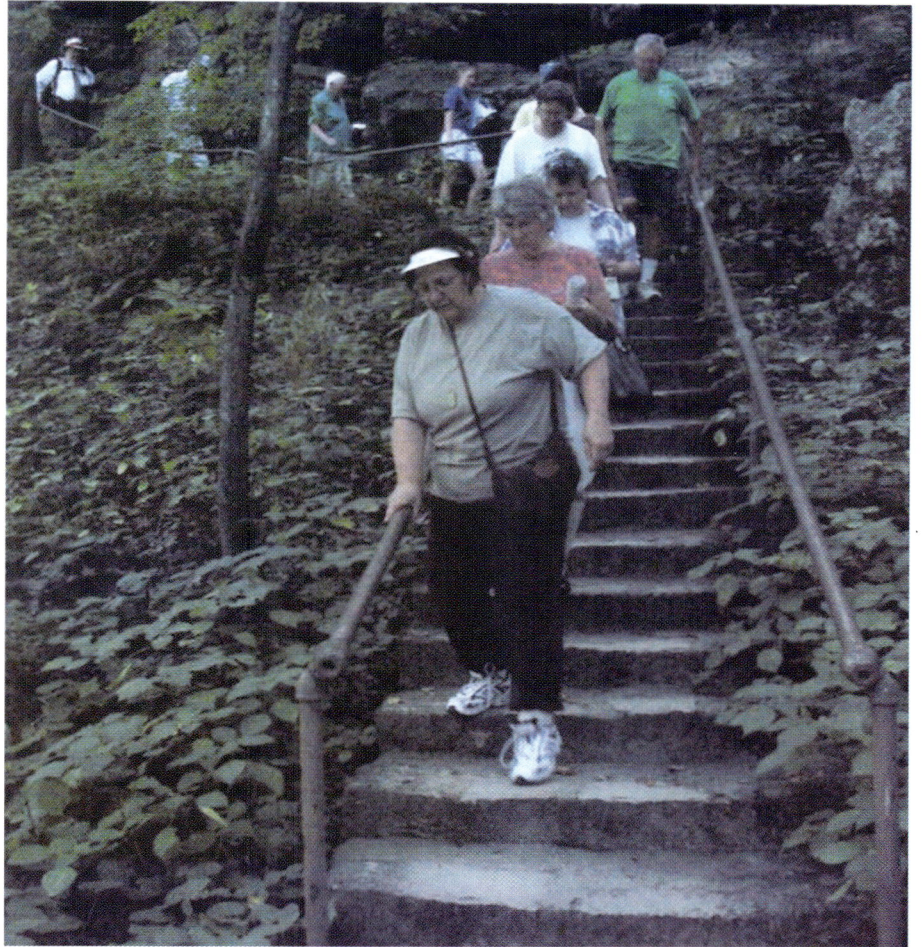

Right: **Stairs to the canyon**
2006
(Jack Madsen Photo)

Below: **Looking into the canyon**
2006
(Jack Madsen Photo)

Left: **Sandstone bluffs in the Minneopa Creek gorge**
1987 (G. Herbst Photo)

Right: **Sandstone face of the canyon wall with burrows of annelids (worms)**
1990 (G. Herbst Photo)

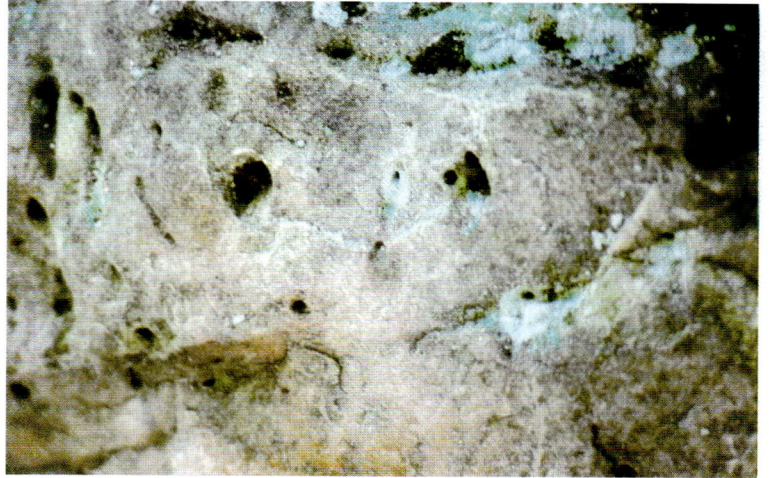

Below: **North canyon wall of the lower Falls**
1999 (G. Herbst Photo)

Above: **Seppman Prairie Bench of the Minnesota River Valley** *1966 (G. Herbst Photo)*
Below: **Diversity of rocks on the prairie** *2003 (G. Herbst Photo)*

Native Americans - Fire and the Big Woods

The coming to America by the early inhabitants is still in question. How, where and when are all questions needing to be answered.

Scientists thought that the migrants who wandered through the central part of the American continent were from Asia. They crossed to America by using a land bridge that existed at that time. Mitochondrial-DNA studies suggest that this migration could have occurred approximately 30,000 years ago at the earliest. It appears that the migration routes were near the west coastal area of the North American continent. The earliest evidence of humans in South America is about 15,000 years ago. It is thought many of the migrants wandered south on the west coast of the North American continent and/or on the east side of the Rocky Mountains.

Most scientists believe that the Native Americans occupied the Minnesota area as the Wisconsin glacier receded about 10,000 years ago. They were nomadic hunters who lived in small social groups and knew how to use fire. They were known for their finely wrought projectile points and were efficient at driving wooly mammoth and giant bison to extinction.

The next dominant group was the Eastern Archaic culture, 7,000 - 3,000 years ago. They were noted for their ground rock and copper tools. They started using small scale cultivation and probably used fire to clear the land.

The Woodland Culture, known for its use of pottery in burial grounds, became prominent in about 1,000 - 1,500 A.D. This culture became prominent because of its extensive use of plant cultivation. The influence of this culture came to Minnesota in about 1,200 A.D. when Indians began using wild rice. It also enabled them to establish permanent settlements. The seasons in Minnesota were not long enough for the corn grown in the south to mature, but wild rice was a very satisfactory substitute.

Glacial erratic at Minneopa 2003 (G. Herbst Photo)

The center of the Mississippian Culture was Cahokia (across the river from present day St. Louis, MO.) This probably included the ancestors of the Dakota Nation.

This increasing population impacted the land and the native's ideas of how the land should be used.

The settler's thoughts of the new land were frightening. They felt this new land needed to be changed from a land infested with "wild animals and savage people" (Luther Standing Bear, Chief of the Ogalala Sioux Indians) to one more civilized. The settlers did not appreciate the changes that had already occurred to the landscape by the Native Americans.

Schoolcraft's records from his 1819 excursion into the Big Sandy Lake area of Minnesota, talked about the landscape.

"Our guides, taking their course by the sun, started into close matted forest of pine and hemlock, through which we urged our way with some difficulty. After traveling two miles, we fell into an Indian path...after pursuing it two miles, we passed through a succession of ponds and marshes, where the mud and water were in some places half leg deep.

These marshes continue four miles and were succeeded by a strip of three miles of open dry sandy barren covered with shrubbery and occasional clumps of pitch pines (Jack Pines). This terminated in a thick forest of hemlock and spruce of young growth, which continued two miles and brought us to the banks of a small lake, with clear water and a pebbly shore. Having no cause to cross, we went to a circuitous route around its shore.

We now again fell into the Indian path. We now entered the great tamarack swamp, in which we progressed about eight miles."

Christopher Columbus Andrews came to

Prairie grass area overgrown with sumac and trees *2003 (G. Herbst Photo)*

Minnesota and the Dakotas in the autumn of 1856 to see the last great wilderness and said, "The trees are of large growth, straight and smooth. Swamps are the exception and are few and far between. The timber land has all the beauty of a sylvan grove.

The entire absence of under brush and decayed logs lends ornament and attraction to the woods. They are more like the groves around a mansion in their neat and cheerful appearance; and awaken reflection on the muses and dialogues of the philosophers rather than apprehension of wild beasts and servants."

Both describe forests different than forests untouched by human hands. Both descriptions suggest frequent burning influenced the landscape. Paintings also suggest a picture consistent with what the essayists tell us.

Eric Grimm reconstructed the Big Woods by using fossil pollen from lake sediments and early records of land surveyors. He found the Big Woods was actually a prairie 5,000 years ago and invaded by oaks 300 years ago.

The Big Woods is a dynamic area which transitioned from dry prairie to xeric oak, through messic basswood-maple environment."

Why transition in the 1600s?

    1. European-Indian contact; with transmission of disease to the Indian population. The Indian population in the region of the Colonies was estimated to be 4,000 to 5,000 in 1634 and dropped to 60 to 150 by 1700.

    2. Native Americans were not around to use fire - this is well documented by letters, travel books and diaries.

    3. Purposes of the use of fire
      a. Travel and hunt easier in the forest.
      b. Encourage young herbaceous growth for forage.
      c. Clear land for agriculture and hunting.

Prairie grass and thickets of American Plum trees *2003 (G. Herbst Photo)*

4. Conversion of the Big Woods to Maple-Basswood forest coincides with the "Little Ice Age" of 1500s to 1700s.

The Europeans thought they were settling the forest primeval when they came in the mid 1800s. The only way to get from St. Paul to the South Bend area was by using the Minnesota River. The water level was so unpredictable that this was unsatisfactory. The wooded area was very wet and trails were non-existent or impossible to find without having an Indian guide.

The land in North America was likely changed by the increasing Indian population and increased agricultural activity.

Rock outcropping of iron conglomerate *2000 (G. Herbst Photo)*

Iron conglomerate *2000 (G. Herbst Photo)*

Above: **The Minneopa prairie viewed from Seppman Mill in 1965** *(G. Herbst Photo)*
Below: **Minnesota River valley view from Seppman Mill in 2003** *(G. Herbst Photo)*

Above: **Prairie grass "Big Blue Stem"** *(Minneopa State Park Photo)*
Below: **Assorted prairie grasses** *(Minneopa State Park Photo)*

Above: **Controlled prairie burn at Minneopa** *2000 (G. Herbst Photo)*
Below: **Ahead of a controlled prairie burn at Minneopa** *2000 (G. Herbst Photo)*

Above: **The blackened prairie after a controlled burn** *2000 (G. Herbst Photo)*
Below: **Regrowth four weeks after the burn** *2000 (G. Herbst Photo)*

Above: **Minneopa prairie with new grass after a burn** *2000 (G. Herbst Photo)*
Below: **Dead oak tree resulted from water flooding** *2001 (G. Herbst Photo)*

Rows of rocks on the prairie that were cleared for a proposed airport runway
2000 (G. Herbst Photo)

**The Seppman Prairie viewed from Pigeon Hill. The rows of rocks
were cleared for an airport runway.** *1948 (G. Herbst Photo)*

Above: **Minneopa Park Expansion Committee (l-r) Fred Lutz, Charlotte Kach, Rod Grove and Ed Peterson** (Lloyd Vollmer Photo)

Left: **A bronze marker, 1977, with names of 142 people who gave $100 or more for the new campground and picnic areas** (G. Herbst Photo)

Minnesota River Valley

Written by Thomas Hughes; *The Daily Review*, Dec. 18, 1899.

Until 1850, the great fertile valley of the Minnesota River was unknown to the civilized world. Fur traders had traversed the region for a century or two in their traffic with the Indians and the trading posts needed to be maintained.

Explorers had written glowing reports about the area, but these were buried in government documents or foreign books which never reached the hands of the ordinary readers and home-seekers.

It was isolated and excluded from the rest of the world by nature. Across the mouth of the Minnesota, 100 miles long and 50 to 60 miles wide, lay a vast forest known as the Big Woods. This formed a barrier to the progress of immigrants.

No explorer had ventured through the tangled woods, lakes and sloughs without an Indian guide. The only way the missionaries could get a wagon through, was by taking it apart and rowing it in a traders boat to Traverse-des-Sioux.

A big freshet occurred in June, 1850, when the Anthony Wayne was in St. Paul. Seeing so much water in the Minnesota River, the captain decided to attempt an excursion up the river on June 28, 1850. The boat ascended as far as the rapids near Carver. This started other boats to try excursions up the river.

These excursions demonstrated the navigability of the Minnesota River. The many people participating in the excursions were completely captivated by the beauty and fertility of the country. With the Treaties of Traverse-des-

The steamboat Lorene with its barge, the O.K. Dubuque, on the Minnesota River at North Mankato *ca. 1910 (Blue Earth Co. Hist. Soc. Photo)*

Sioux and Mendota, whereby the Indians ceded over to the United States all of southern and central Minnesota west of the Mississippi. As soon as the Treaties were signed, the settlers poured in and several cities in this area were founded in 1852.

There are wonderful stories of the abundance of the fish in the streams. It seems all one had to do was cut a willow switch, go to the waters edge and whistle. A piscatorial monster a yard or two long would walk up your line and open their mouths and gills so you could insert the switch easily.

The numbers of fish caught depended simply on the length of the switch. It is claimed many weighed 500 pounds (No written records available?)

Grapevine covered trees along the north bank of the Minnesota River *2002 (G. Herbst Photo)*

The Minnesota River with its many snags in the stream bed *2002 (G. Herbst Photo)*

Right: **South Bend townsite** *2002*
(G. Herbst Photo)

Below: **Along the shore of the Minnesota River just east of the South Bend townsite** *2002*
(G. Herbst Photo)

Left: **The beauty of the Minnesota River** *2002* *(G. Herbst Photo)*

Below: **Minnesota River near the mouth of Minneopa Creek at low water** *1997* *(G. Herbst Photo)*

View of the Minnesota River from campgrounds *2003 (Minneopa State Park Photo)*

Minnesota River with its boulders and obstructions *1976 (G. Herbst Photo)*

Minnesota River Regatta
1963 (G. Herbst Photo)

Minnesota River in winter *(Minneopa State Park Photo)*

Minnesota River above Minneopa Creek *(Minneopa State Park Photo)*

Seppman Mill

In May 1929, one and one-fourth acres were deeded to the Blue Earth County Historical Society by Alfred and Martha Seppman. This land included the Seppman mill and granary which was built 1862-1864. The mill was wind driven; the first one to be built in the vicinity and in 1929 thought to be the only stone mill in Minnesota.

The mill was completed and started grinding in 1864. It is 33 feet in diameter at the base and 20 feet in diameter at the top. The walls at the bottom are two feet thick. The rocks came from the surrounding countryside. The mill was 30 feet above ground. There were four arms, each 35 feet long. The arms were connected using a hub. The roof was dome shaped and hung on a center shaft, so it could be turned to face the direction of the wind. There were stairs on the inside and the outside, with a platform near the roof to make mechanical adjustments.

The cogs and hubs of the wheels were hand hewn from hard maple wood which was harvested from the area. The grist stones were on the second floor and were hand polished by the workmen. Operating capacity of the mill was 150 bushels of wheat per day.

The mill was used until June 3, 1873, when it was hit by lightening and two of the arms were destroyed. The two arms were not replaced and the mill was used until 1880 with just two arms.

The mill ground no more flour because other mills were operating with newer equipment and

The Seppman Mills - posing are (l-r) Herman Seppman, unidentified, Willie Seppman (son of Herman and Christina Hanel Seppman), Emma (Seppman) Grice, Henry and Chas. Seppman
1900 (Dorothy Paulson Photo)

were strong competitors. The mill was used to grind feed for livestock until 1890 when another windstorm damaged the mill. This time it was not repaired.

The mill was restored by J.B. Nelson Co. in 1929. More restoration was done in 1969. The exterior surface had been covered with cement in the 1930s. This was later removed and the exterior appeared as it did originally.

A new home was built for the Seppmans in the 1870s and their old home, a stone building just below the mill, was used as a warehouse for the mill.

The room on the mill that was used for bolting the flour was torn down in 1913.

In later years, the mill was hidden from view by trees and there was no designated road to the mill.

The Minnesota State Highway Department built a roadside parking area near the Seppman Mill off Highway 68 in 1955-1956.

Visitors wanted better access to the area. The parking area was vacated in the early 1970s and regraded in the next road repair.

Seppman Mill - On the left is the stone grist mill and a granary built by Louis Seppman. On the right side are the remnants of the wooden mill.
1900 (Dorothy Paulson Photo)

Seppman Mill
1986 (G. Herbst Photo)

Left: **Seppman Mill in 1929**
(Jordan Kagermeier Photo)

Right: **Seppman Mill in 1969**
(G. Herbst Photo)

Seppman homestead
2003 (G. Herbst Photo)

Seppman Mill and stone granary after restoration in 1986
(G. Herbst Photo)

Left and below:
The Seppman Mill Granary
1986 (G. Herbst Photo)

Above: **Wooden gear inside the Seppman Mill** *2000 (G. Herbst Photo)*

Below: **Millstones and wooden gears inside Seppman Mill** *1986 (G. Herbst Photo)*

Above: **Seppman Mill marker on Highway 68** *2003 (G. Herbst Photo)*

Below: **Aerial view shows the Seppman Mill, house and roadside parking area as it looked in 1969** *(G. Herbst Photo)*

Left: **Bench in Seppman Mill observation area**
(Minneopa State Park Photo)

Below: **Bench in the mill area with a view of the prairie area**
(Minneopa State Park Photo)

The Minneopa Brand

Through the years, the name "Minneopa" was used by a number of different businesses. Several examples are shown on the following pages.

1½ Ounces Net Wt.

TURMERIC

PACKED FOR
L. PATTERSON MERC. CO.
MANKATO, MINN.

Above: **Minneopa Brand Corn Syrup**
(Blue Earth Co. Hist. Soc. Photo)
Right: **Minneopa Brand Turmeric and uses for the spice** *(Blue Earth Co. Hist. Soc. Photo)*
Below: **Minneopa Brands**
(Blue Earth Co. Hist. Soc. Photo)

TURMERIC
FRESH SPICES ADD FINER FLAVOR!
SPICE FLAVOR HINTS
(Note: Season to taste — just a pinch or sprinkle.)

CINNAMON: Apple dumplings, sliced bananas, puddings, apple fritters.
NUTMEG: Veal stew, spinach, apple sauce, bread dumplings, custard.
CLOVES: Chocolate dessert or sauce, baked beans, baked apples.
MUSTARD POWDER: Sauces, gravies, canned corn, salad dressings.
WHITE PEPPER: Salads, cream soups, white sauces.
CHILI POWDER: Soups, meat sauces, spaghetti sauce, scrambled eggs, french dressing.
CELERY SALT: Soups, salad dressings, tomato juice, cold meats, boiled eggs.

Above: **Novelty glassware was sold in the local liquor stores** *(Jordan Kagermeier Photo)*

Above: **Minneopa Brand Rolled Oats** (Blue Earth Co. Hist. Soc. Photo)

Left: **Minneopa Brand - L. Patterson Mercantile, Mankato, Minnesota** *(Jordan Kagermeier Photo)*

Below: **Minneopa Brand Pasteurized Loaf Cheese** *(Mary Lou Ihrke Photo)*

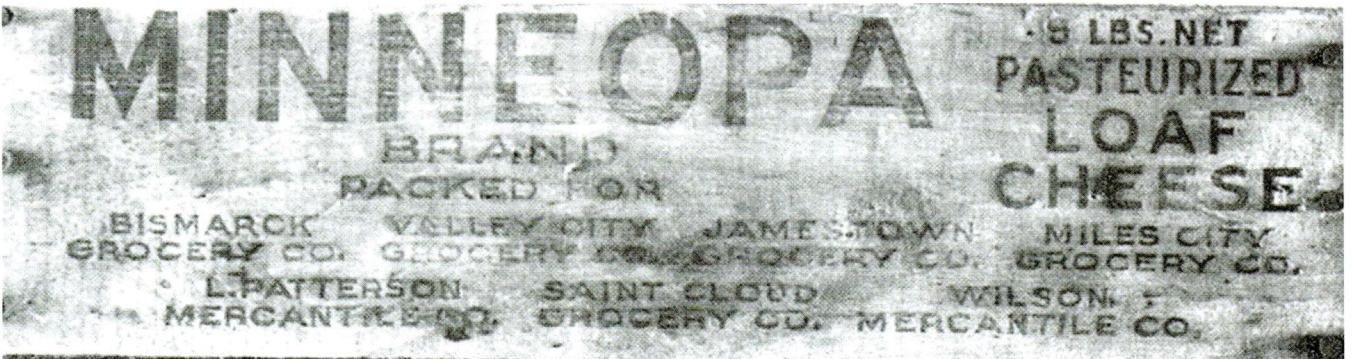

Free Press Printing Co.

Printers - Publishers - Binders - Stationers

DAILY and WEEKLY
FREE PRESS

The Largest Printing Plant
in Southern Minnesota

MINNEOPA STATE PARK —NEAR MANKATO

County, Office and Bank Supplies

Above: **Free Press Printing business card** *ca. 1915* *(Blue Earth Co. Hist. Soc. Photo)*
Below: **Minneopa Garage post card** *ca. 1914* **This building still stands at the corner
of Cherry and Second Streets in Mankato** *(Blue Earth Co. Hist. Soc. Photo)*

Minneopa Garage, Second and Cherry St., Mankato, Minn.

Flora and Fauna

Minneopa is populated with a diverse mix of woodland, prairie and wetland plant and animal life. Some of those are featured on the following pages.

Above: **Bloodroot**
Below: **Bloodroot in flower**
    (G. Herbst Photos)

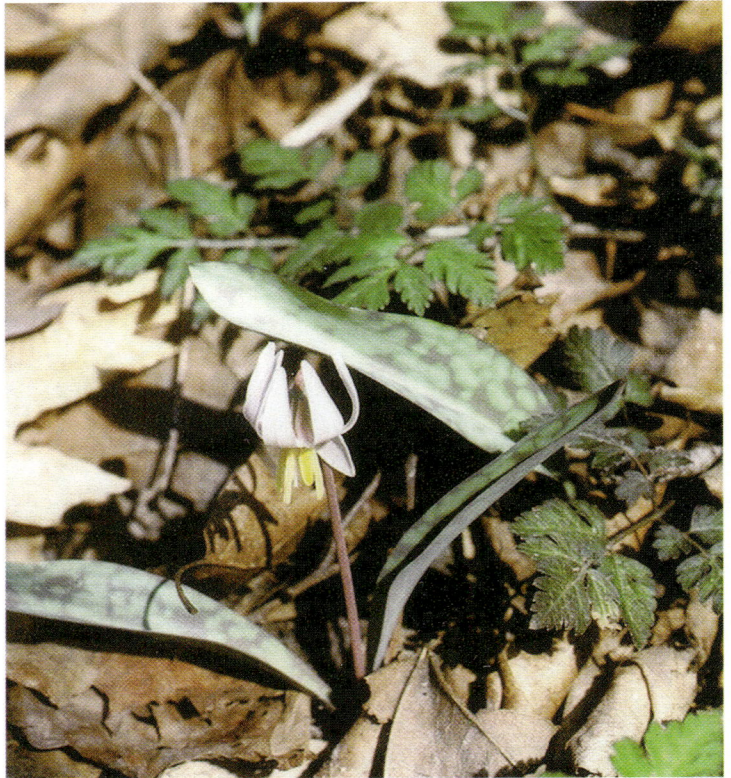

Right: **White Trout Lily (Erythronium Albidum)**
1987 (G. Herbst Photo)

Below: **Dutchman's Breeches and Bloodroots in flower**
1987 (G. Herbst Photo)

Yellow Lady Slipper Orchids (Cypripedium calceolus) *1966 (G. Herbst Photos)*

Above: **Pasqueflower
(Anemone patens)**
1982 (G. Herbst Photo)

Right: **Bottle Gentian
(Gentiana andrewsii)**
2001 (G. Herbst Photo)

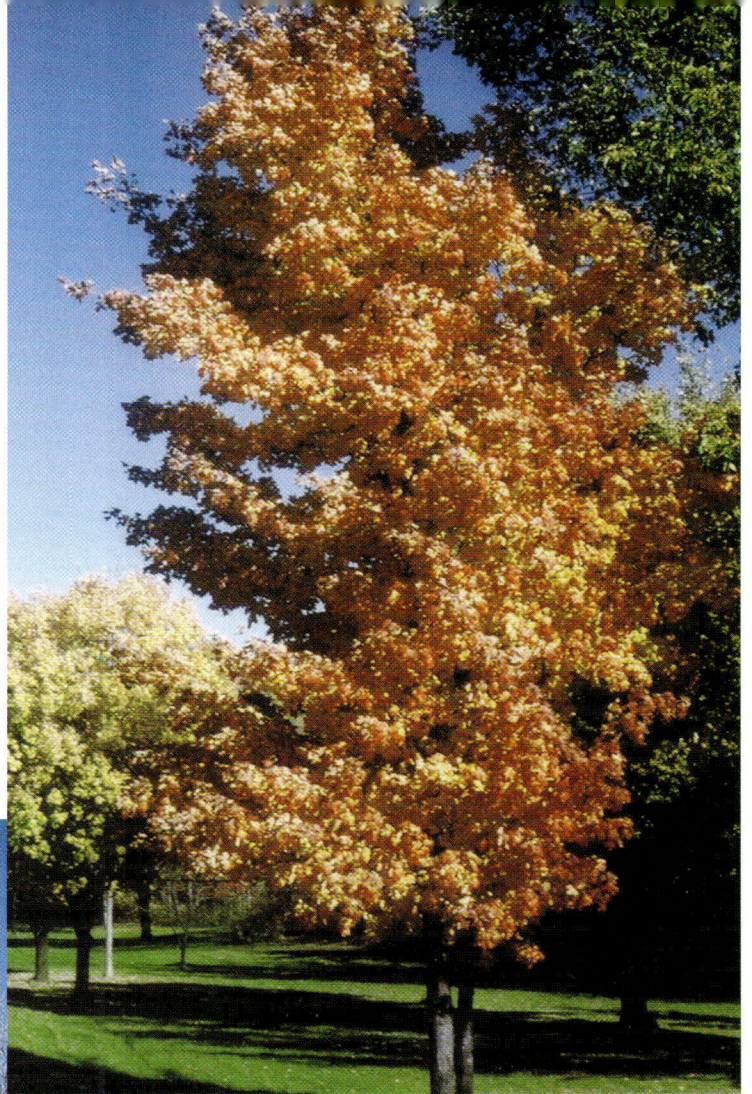

Right: **Young maple trees show their beautiful fall colors** (G. Herbst Photo)

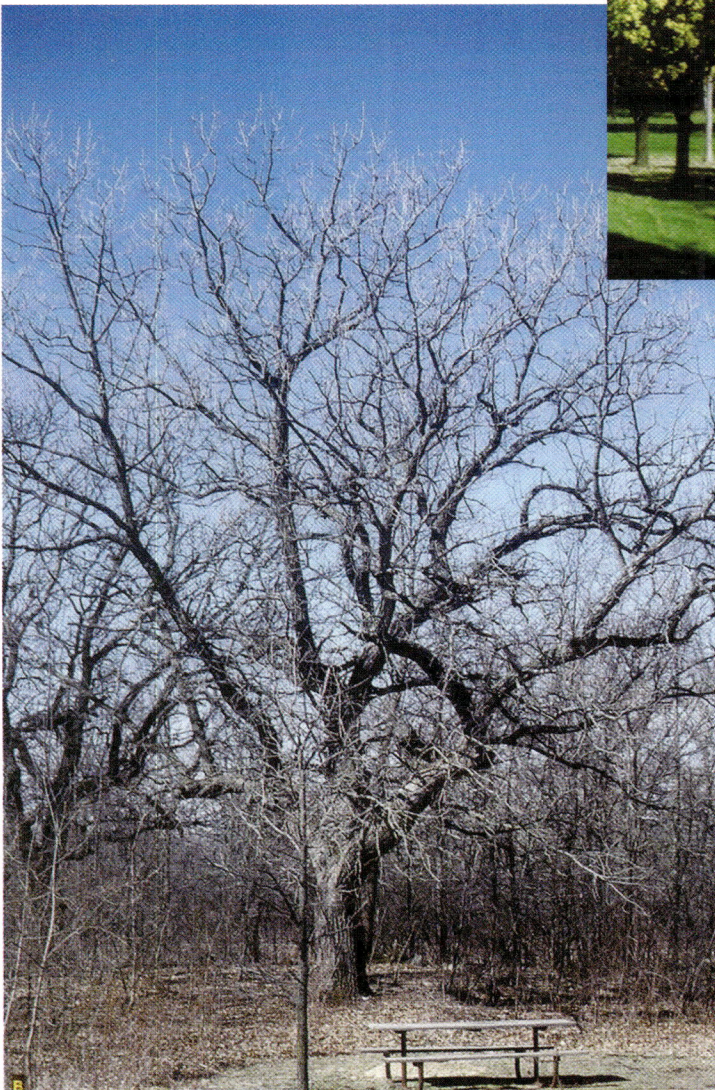

Left: **Large burr oak tree in the campground** 2003 (G. Herbst Photo)

Above: **A stand of poplar trees used as a food source by beaver**
2004 (G. Herbst Photo)

Right: **Remains of a poplar tree being harvested by a beaver**
2001 (G. Herbst Photo)

76

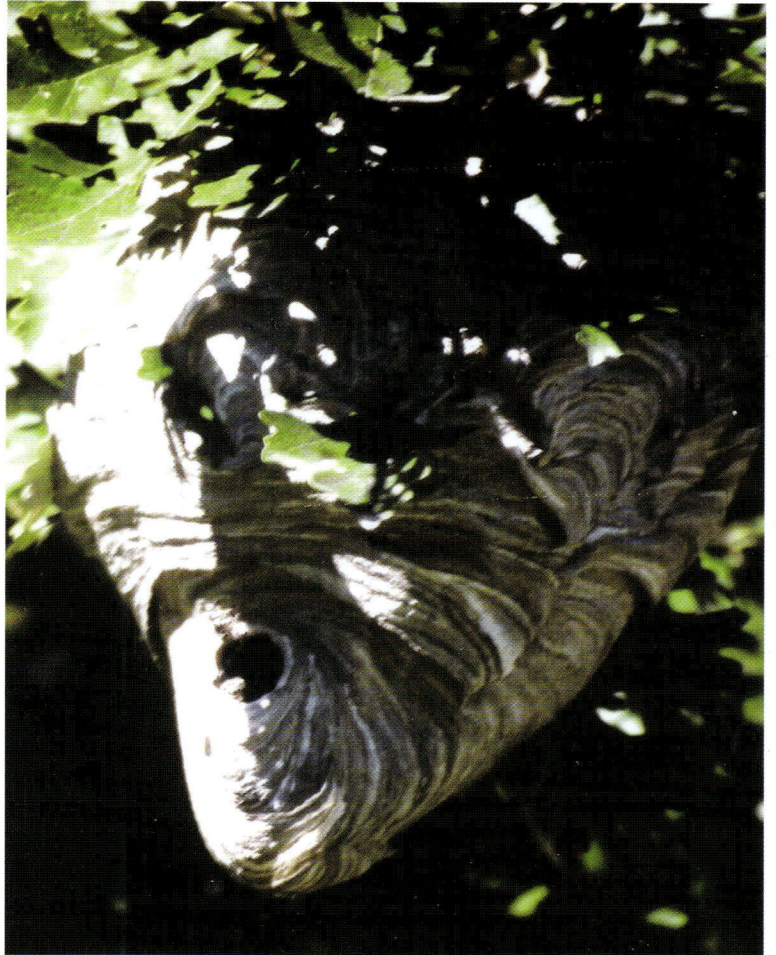

Right: **Hornet nest resting in an oak tree in the camping area of the Park**
(*G. Herbst Photo*)

Below: **G.M. Palmer Walnut Grove**
(*G. Herbst Photo*)

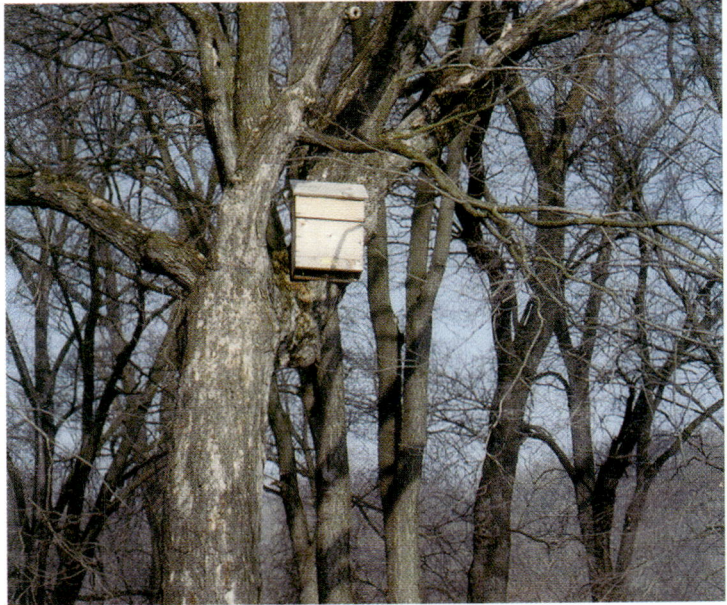

Right: **A bat house has been mounted in a basswood tree at the picnic shelter** *2003 (G. Herbst Photo)*

Below: **Participants in the annual bird survey of Minneopa (l-r) Brand Frentz, Tim Grant, L. Filter, Linda Milo-Riedall, Gordon Herbst, Mary Hollingsworth, Ruth Rankin** *2000 (Jeff Thompson Photo)*

Passenger Pigeons

I remember the older senior citizens of the area talking about the great numbers of pigeons which filled the skies, sometimes with several layers of birds.

I grew up in South Bend, which is adjacent to Minneopa State Park and Pigeon Hill, but do not remember any comments about pigeons and why the hill was named Pigeon Hill.

It was while researching the history of Minneopa State Park that I came across an article written by Davis P. Mackley. It was to his old friends Mr. and Mrs. David P. Davis, on the occasion of their Golden Anniversary in 1882. He recollects the naming of the geologic features of the area and also states that on smoky Indian summer days, the air was filled with wild pigeons. He comments that it seemed like millions of pigeons would pass over a point in one day in South Bend, MN.

The passenger pigeon was probably the most abundant bird in the New World. The earliest descriptions, which date back nearly 300 years, state that the pigeon traveled in flocks of hundreds of millions. It was chiefly found in eastern North America, estimated at 3 – 5 billion birds, accounting for nearly one fourth of all North American birds.

In their early history, the pigeons wintered from the Ohio Valley southward, principally from Arkansas and North Carolina to Florida, Louisana and parts of Texas. The early history of pigeons in the Upper Mississippi River was recorded by the French in 1680.

Serious scientific studies on the pigeons were not done. Much of our information are fragments gleaned from personal accounts which are incomplete and sometimes contradictory.

Passenger pigeons migrated early in the spring season, often as soon as the ground was without snow. The arrival dates of the first birds had little bearing on when the main flights would migrate. The earliest arrival date in southern Minnesota was March 9, 1878.

The spring migration often passed over in three or four days, rarely lasting more than a month. Since 1880, the large spring flocks stopped coming to Minnesota and there are no reliable records of identification after 1895.

The passenger pigeon in Minnesota was an abundant summer resident over the entire state with breeding occurring by isolated pairs and sporadically in large colonies.

Several nestings occurred in Minnesota in the years of 1864, 1867 and 1877, but accounts are poorly recorded. The last nesting activity occurring in Minnesota was near Minneapolis in 1895. The nesting in Minnesota which occurred in 1877 was disturbed by firing shotguns in the nesting areas which would cause the birds to rise by the thousands and when repeated, they would leave the nest/squab and never return.

The wild pigeon (passenger pigeon) had a habit of nesting in very large colonies, containing hundreds of thousands or maybe millions of birds packed in forests 30 – 40 miles long and 3 to 10 miles wide. The area was approximately 150,000 acres and the nesting covered 100,000 acres with nearly every tree having some nests and up 110 nests in some trees. The majority of nests were built only of small twigs loosely placed so that the egg could be seen from the ground.

Incubation was shared by both parents. The male covered the nest from 10:00 a.m. to 3:00 p.m., at which time the female came to cover the nest. The incubation time was 12 – 13 days. If an egg did not hatch within a few hours after the incubation time, the nest was abandoned, even if the egg was cracked and the chick was appearing.

The writings of Audubon and Alexander Wilson report in 1806, that birds returning from their feeding grounds were flying with steadiness and rapidity above gunshot range in several strata deep and so close together that one shot would bring down several birds.

The birds filled the sky with equal density from horizon to horizon for nearly four hours. Wilson estimated that 2,230,272,000 birds had passed and felt that was a conservative estimate. These were birds that had been feeding and were relieving an equal number of birds that were-waiting for their relief. Estimates of mast (nuts, acorns, etc.) required to feed the birds one day was 17,424,400 bushels.

Audubon attempted similar calculations on an autumn day in 1813 in Kentucky and arrived at 1,150,136,000 bushels to feed the birds for just one day.

Utilization of the pigeon population included a source of human food. Some people considered the pigeon flesh to be very tasty. However some Indians said they preferred the flesh of skunks to that of pigeons.

The birds were eaten fresh, dried or smoked. Longer term preservation was accomplished by packing roasted birds in casks and covering them with molten fat to exclude the air. The meat would keep for months. Pickling, salting or packing the meat in spiced apple cider in sealed jars were also methods of preservation.

The fat of pigeons was used for many purposes. The squabs had large amounts of body fat which was rendered and used as sweet butter that would not deteriorate for one year. There was extensive feeding of the pigeons to hogs and the feathers were used in large quantities for bedding. Bird lime (excrement) contributed to building good soil.

Harvesting the pigeons developed into an organized business in a relatively short time. Men went about with sticks tipping squabs out of their nests while others were clubbing them to death. Other men chopped down trees, causing the squabs to fall to the ground so they could be harvested. On sand bluffs, flocks of pigeons flew so low that they were clubbed to the ground and gathered.

The commerce in pigeons did not become important until the railroad afforded rapid transportation to the big cities. The birds were killed, dressed and put in barrels with ice. Others were netted and shipped live to be used for trap shooting and others were "stall fed" birds which were used for later marketing.

Telegraphers transmitted the information about locations of the colonies, which allowed many pigeoners to work in one area and disrupt the nesting of a large number of birds. Shotgunners joined in the disruption of the nesting sites which further aggravated the decline of the birds.

An interesting habit of the passenger pigeon impacting agriculture was the disgorging of the crop when it found food more to its liking. It was believed that pigeon grass was efficiently distributed in Michigan by the pigeons disgorging the seeds in the wheat fields which was more desirable to the pigeon. The digestive process was rapid, however, and it is questioned if any of the disgorged seeds would have actually germinated in the fields.

Cultivated grains were eaten by the birds. Buckwheat and wheat were high priorities on the edible list of the passenger pigeon, followed by barley, rye, oats, corn, hemp and peas. Animal foods included earthworms, insects, caterpillars and snails.

The time the passenger pigeons may have been the most destructive was at seeding time, before the kernels were covered with soil. With the advent of grain drills, the seed was covered immediately and the damage to agriculture by the pigeon was relatively small. Pigeons were not as destructive later in the season when the ripened fields were standing or when the grain was shocked.

Various methods were used to scare the birds away and the grain could be treated with saltpeter, creosote, and rolled in lime, ashes or smoked over a fire.

The fall migration in the northern states began the end of August with the main flights during the first two weeks of September. These pigeons were reported to swarm down on and cover wheat fields. Sometimes nets were set up and hundreds of birds could be caught.

Legislation for the protection of the pigeon was not easily enacted because it was thought that "the passenger pigeon needs no protection." It was thought that the pigeon would never be exterminated as long as large forests remained. Furthermore, it was considered no more cruel to kill pigeons than it was domestic animals in stockyard killings.

Areas that did enact legislation could not enforce the laws.

The decline of the passenger pigeons was rapid. The steepest decline was in the 1870s. They were scarce by the 1880s and rare in the 1890s. The bird disappeared from the wild in about 1900. The sole survivor of the once great population died about 10 years later in captivity. The passenger pigeon was gone forever.

Park Buildings and Campground

Above: **Works Project Administration (WPA) constructing stairs to the canyon in the 1930s** *(Minneopa State Park Photo)*

Below: **WPA construction in the 1930s** *(Minneopa State Park Photo)*

Right: **The former kitchen in Minneopa State Park** *2001* *(G. Herbst Photo)*

Below: **A park pavillion that was built in 1914** *2000* *(G. Herbst Photo)*

Left: **Steps into the Minneopa canyon built by WPA workers in the late 1930s**
1999 (G. Herbst Photo)

Below: **Picnic shelter and wellhouse**
2003 (G. Herbst Photo)

Above: **The Nature Center (formerly the kitchen) on the left and the kiosk and wellhouse on the right**
Below: **The kitchen (now the Nature Center) had four wood cook stoves for public use**
2003 (G. Herbst Photos)

Above: **Picnic shelter in upper Park, built in 1967 and removed in 2003**
(G. Herbst Photo)

Below: **Latrine built by WPA in the 1930s** *(G. Herbst Photo)*

**Former Contact Station
for the Falls area**
1998 (G. Herbst Photo)

Park Office
1999
(G. Herbst Photo)

**Campground
Contact Station**
2003 (G. Herbst Photo)

Above and below: **Camper Cabin at Minneopa State Park** *2003 (G. Herbst Photos)*

Park Activities

Above: **Gathering ripened seeds from native plants** 2005 *(Harry Meyering Center Photo)*

Left: **Threshing seeds from wildflowers, Harry Meyering Center residents and supervisors** 2005 *(Harry Meyering Center Photo)*

Ice climbing *(Minneopa State Park Photos)*

Winter fun during "Snow Day" *(Minneopa State Park Photos)*

Blue Earth County Historical Society History Club
2006 (Jack Madsen Photos)

Wedding in the Park
(Minneopa State Park Photos)

**Volleyball games and sack races are some of the
many activities that take part at Minneopa State Park**
(Minneopa State Park Photos)

Left: **Centennial visitors waiting for treats**
2005 (Tim Pulis Photo)

Below: **Minneopa Centennial Birthday Cake** *2005*
(Tim Pulis Photo)

Appendix

Management at Minneopa State Park

Minneopa State Park was the third state park to be established,
preceded only by Itasca and Dalles of the St. Croix.

Managers:

J.B. Hodges	1906 to May 1907
	He had previously been Minneopa Railroad Depot Agent
William R. Williams	May 1907 to December 1913
Clarence Williams	April 1914 to April 1915
	He was the son of William Williams
John W. Roberts	April 1915 to March 1921
John Ellis	March 1921 to December 1935
Robert Ulmen	January 1936 to October 1939
Garfield James	October 1939 to May 1951
Carl Pederson	May 1951 to March 1963
Lester Larson	April 1963 to June 1965
Oscar Swanson	July 1965 to August 1973
John Lee	August 1973 to April 1976
Walter Benson	April 1976 to October 1977
Howard O. Ward	October 1977 to Present

Assistant Managers:

Craig Berberich	June 1975 to June 1976
Arol McCaslin	November 1976 to November 1976
Walter Hohn	May 1977 to August 1978
Bob Johnson	September 1978 to December 1978
Mike Tonder	January 1979 to May 1980
Doug Midtke	June 1980 to July 1980
Dan Roth	August 1980 to July 1988
Gary Teipel	September 1988 to September 2001
Joel Groebner	December 2002 to April 2003
Elaine Feikema	March 2003 to March 2004
Craig Beckman	September 2004 to June 2006
Steve Rose	July 2006 to Present

Minneopa Creek Headwaters and Watershed

Minneopa Creek begins in western Blue Earth County in a wetland area which was "ditched" in the 1930s, so the higher areas could be used for agriculture.

Lieberg Lake and Strom Lake are the headwaters for the portion of the creek which has been channelized and flows into Lily Lake. The outlet for Loon Lake and Mills Lake near Lake Crystal flows into Crystal Lake. This provides water for the creek, a short distance from the outlet of Lily Lake.

The Minneopa Creek Watershed collects water from portions of Butternut Valley Township, Lincoln Township, Garden City Township, Judson Township and South Bend Township in Blue Earth County. Minneopa Creek also collects water from the City of Lake Crystal and four square miles of land in eastern Brown County. The creek is part of the Middle Minnesota River Watershed, which is part of the Mississippi River Basin.

Restoration of some natural areas is underway. The connection of fragmented ecosystems and floodplain stabilization provides space for additional activities.

Minneopa Creek Watershed

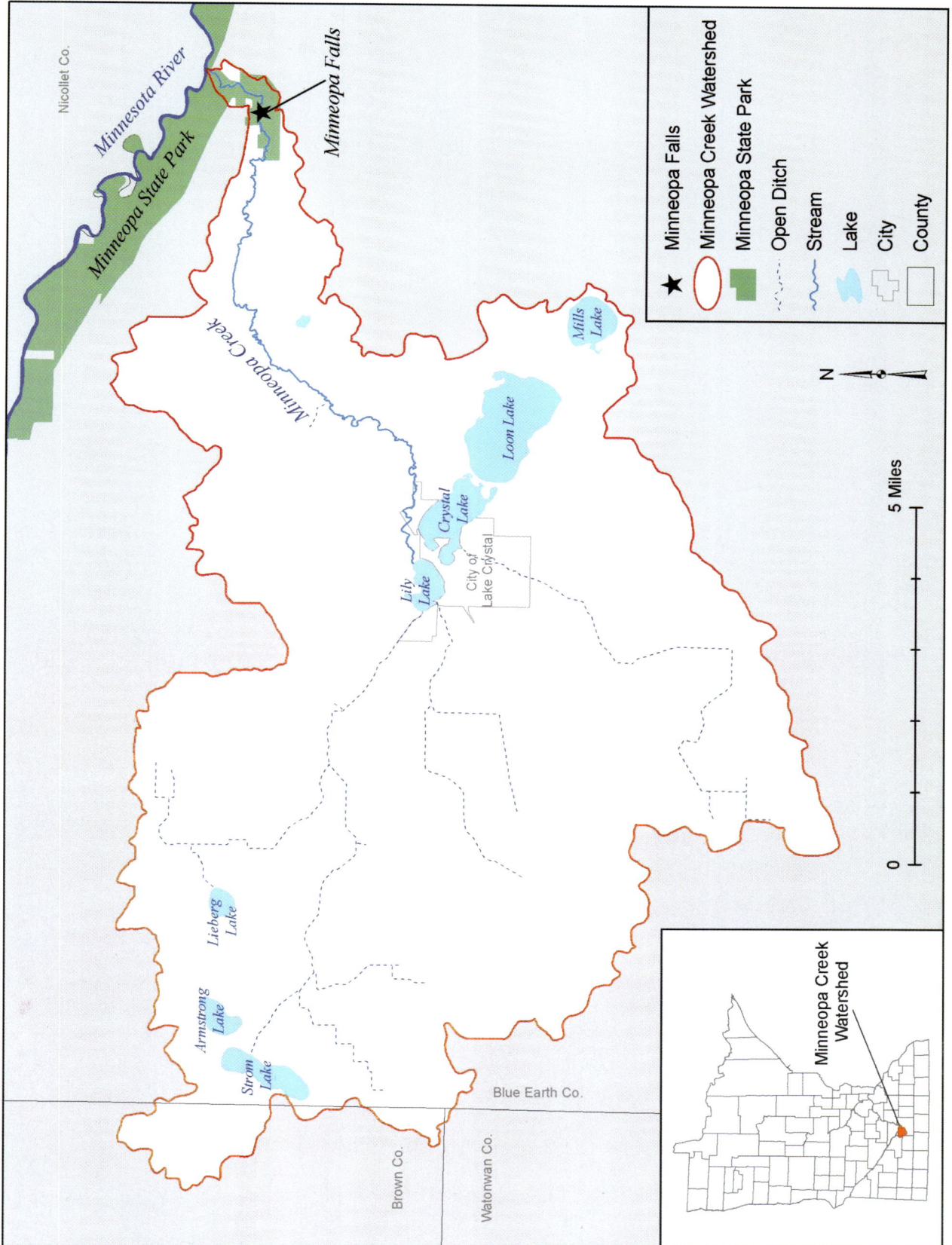

Nicollet Co.

Minnesota River

Minneopa State Park

Minneopa Falls

Minneopa Falls

Minneopa Creek

Mills Lake

Loon Lake

Crystal Lake

Lily Lake

City of Lake Crystal

Lieberg Lake

Armstrong Lake

Strom Lake

Blue Earth Co.

Brown Co.

Watonwan Co.

Legend

★ Minneopa Falls
◯ Minneopa Creek Watershed
▨ Minneopa State Park
⋯ Open Ditch
〜 Stream
▧ Lake
⬚ City
▢ County

N

5 Miles

0

Minneopa Creek Watershed

Minneopa Area 1865
Blue Earth County, Minnesota

Points of Interest

a Seppman Mill
b Seppman Mill House
c Seppman Farm Buildings
d Seppman Airport Hanger
e Seppman Airport
f Morgan Saw Mill, c1940's
g Morgan Saw Mill, c1960's
h Ulmen Building Site
i Ball Field
j Campground 1940's-50's
k Lyons Saw Mill
l Rifle Range
m Minneopa Park Hotel

South Bend

Minneopa State Park

1:56,036

Roads
Pigeon Hill
Townsites
Lyons Creek
Blue Earth River
Points of Interest
Indian Village

Minneopa Park Chronology

1700 10/1   LeSueur arrived in our area

       10/14   Fort LeHillier built

1702   Fort LeHillier abandoned

1848   Henry H. Sibley, delegate to Congress from
           Wisconsin Territory

1849 3/3   Gov. Alexander Ramsey arrives at Mendota and
           declares Minnesota Territory duly organized

           H.H. Sibley elected a delegate to Congress for the
           Territory of Minnesota

       7/18   Steamboat "Anthony Wayne" ascended Minnesota River
           to near Traverse des Sioux

       7/25   Steamboat "Yankee" goes beyond the Blue Earth River
           on the Minnesota River

1850 7/22   "Yankee" steamer goes beyond Mankato

1851 7/18   Traverse des Sioux Treaty concluded

1852 – 1870   Steamboat Period

1852 6/8   Pierre River renamed Minnesota River

       3/5   Blue Earth County created by Territorial Legislature

1853 6/?   "Clarion" landed at South Bend bank of the Minnesota River

       7/?   Isaac S. Lyons and family came to South Bend

       8/1   D.C. Evans and Lyman Mathews came to South Bend

       8/6   Lyons moved to Minneopa Creek and built a cabin there

       ?/?   South Bend Co. accepted D.C. Evans and Mathews,
           E.R. May and Owen Herbert

       ?/?   Survey of South Bend; D.T. Turpin

       ?/?   Capt. Reno surveying military road - Dodd

       12/26   D.C. Evans laid foundation for his 3 story house in
           South Bend

1854 7/1   Government survey starts in Blue Earth County

       8/8   South Bend consists of 5 houses and 26 inhabitants

       ?/?   L.D. Mills came to Minnesota

       ?/?   South Bend adjoins Clarion City; Lyon's Creek Sawmill

       ?/?   D.C. Evans built his 3 story house in South Bend

       8/8   Lyons started his sawmill on the Minneopa Creek

       9/9   John Lyons, son of Isaac, first white death in South Bend

1855 6/14   Work started on military road from South Bend to Mendota

       8/20   Work started on Blue Earth River bridge from Mankato
           to South Bend

       ?/?   South Bend school started

1857 6/5   Daniel Buck settled in South Bend

       8/1   Three stage lines operating in Mankato

1857		LeHillier platted
1858	3/20	South Bend village incorporated
1858		Minnesota becomes a state in the United States of America
1859	1/5	Daily mail service from St. Paul to South Bend and Mankato
	7/27	Mr. Hill photographs Minneopa
	8/15	Mr. Whitney photographs Minneopa Falls
	?/?	Miner Porter built Summer Resort in South Bend
1860	5/19	St. Peter & Traverse residents picnic at Minneopa
	10/26	South Bend Mills started, largest in county
	11/30	Valley Stage Lines brings mail
	12/6	Porter running Minneinneopa House
1861	4/10	Minnesota River higher than in 1853 or 1859
	11/1	First Blue Earth County Fair at South Bend
	9/?	Ginseng trade from Blue Earth County
		83,000 Pounds @ 0.08 = $6,640.00
	?/?	Minnesota Regiment of Volunteers goes to the Civil War
1862	?/?	Great Flood; snow = 4 feet
	4/?	Flood waters carry away the government bridge over the Blue Earth River
		Sioux Indian Uprising
	8/8	Sioux attack Lower Sioux Agency
	8/23	New Ulm attacked by the Indians
	11/7	Indians sentenced to die, transported to Camp Lincoln in West Mankato
	12/26	38 Sioux Indians hanged in Mankato
1863	4/?	Sod fort built at Judson
1864	2/6	Warehouse built at Minneopa
1865	5/17	Blue Earth County offers a bounty for hostile Indian scalp
1866	5/21	Mr. Harley & Mr. Nason photograph Minneopa
	7/2	Minnesota Stage Coach to Blue Earth Valley
	7/28	Phillip Tounar operates windmill, just above South Bend – excellent flour
1866		Omaha RR built to Belle Plaine
1867		Belle Plaine to LeSueur
1868		LeSueur to Mankato
1869		Mankato to Lake Crystal
1870		Lake Crystal to St. James
1871		St. James to Worthington
1872		Worthington to Sioux City
1867	5/10	"Julia" steamboat sank in Minnesota River
	5/18	W.W. Davis moves store back to South Bend from Mankato

1867	8/3	Mr. Wall photographs Minneopa; also Mr. Beebe
1868	6/27	M. Porter refits "Minneopa Park" with plants etc.
	10/?	St. Paul & Sioux City Railroad reaches Mankato
1868	10/17	Northwestern Telegraph Co. completes installation of lines
1869	9/18	Blue Earth River bridge completed
	9/25	Universalist Sunday School picnic at Minneopa
	9/25	Col. Smith moves his ferry on Blue Earth River at LeHillier to Jones Ford
	12/8	St. Paul & Sioux City Railroad reaches Lake Crystal
	?/?	Buck, Sowers & Co. starts a stoneware manufacturing company in South Bend
1870	?/?	Porter's Summer Resort abandoned
	1/15	Winona Road completed to Mankato
	3/1	Warehouse built by railroad depot at Minneopa
	3/1	D.C. Evans lays out town at Minneopa
	6/19	Presley Church excursion at Minneopa Falls
	6/2	St. Peter residents have picnic at Minneopa
	9/19	Minneopa Townsite platted
1871	1/3	Robt. Goodyear buys 34 acres from Y.B. Yopts for a nursery
1873	1/7,8,9	Polar wave sweeps Minnesota
	?/?	Grasshopper invasion; continues for 5 seasons
		Grasshoppers destroy crops
1874	2/6	Stone wall found on Lewis Kemnitz's farm in Nicollet Co.
1876	6/15	St. James Sunday School picnic at Minneopa
	6/30	Barrot House renamed Minneopa House by Porter
	9/7	James and Younger Gang seen in Mankato area
	9/7	Northfield Bank attacked by James/Younger Gang
1877	6/14	Camp meetings at Minneopa
	11/15	Earthquake in Mankato area
1878	5/22	Camp meetings of ME conference at Minneopa
	6/20	Lyons Creek bridge built
1879	11/?	Grain Elevator built at Minneopa
	3/22	Sioux City Railroad builds culvert over Minneopa Creek
	6/22	Camp meeting - 5,000 people at Minneopa
1880	3/5	New bridge over Minnesota River completed
1881	3/2	Residence and store of Rev. D. Rowlands burned at Minneopa Townsite
		Milwaukee Railroad to Mankato
1882	6/16	Camp meeting at Minneopa
1888	6/1	Machinery to Minneopa to drill for gas
1888-1889		Artesian well

1889	Riverside Park Addition, S.C. & G. Pond, adjoins LeHillier on west
1890s	Miner Porter's Resort purchased by W.W.P. McConnell & Mrs. Swan - used for dairy herd of Jersey cattle
1891 5/12	Wm. E. Williams, weigh master, deputy at Minneopa
1893	Jewett murder
1893 5/16	Blood Hounds investigate after Jewett murder
1897 10/5	A. Lincoln Store and Post Office burned in South Bend
1898	Pigeon Hill road improved by county
1899 10/2	Railroad work camp broken up
5/24	New railroad
1900 11/11	South Bend Hotel and Store burn
4/4	Railroad crew finished rip rapping along Minneopa Creek
1905	Minneopa State Park legislated into existence
	Railroad culvert built
1906 2/1	Old McConnell farm house burned
8/7	Cut made west of Minneopa Depot; new depot 100 ft. east of original depot
	Minneopa Creek bridge built near station
11/26	Railroad Station #2 built
1906-7	70 acres bought by State of Minnesota
1907	Iron fence built around the Falls
	New cement stairway to ravine
	Railing along embankment
	New picnic tables added to Park
1914 5/29	Stake out Minneopa Pavillion
9/23	Request for store in Park by J.W. Roberts and Charles R. Fisher
	Kitchen present in Minneopa State Park
	Wall of concrete near north iron fence
	Wall built to stop erosion along fence
1919	Wire fence along top of ledge, 120 feet
	Iron fence along Falls repaired
	High water washed out bridge below the Falls
	New stove for the kitchen
1921	Cement Arch Bridge built by Senctor Constr. Co. of Minneapolis - $2,200.00
	Appropriation for pavilion improvement - $700
	Install more swings - $400
1924	Pavilion, 2 wings added by J.B. Nelson & Co.
1927 1/20	Lyons Creek concrete culvert 20 x 10 ft.

1927	8/4	Widen road through Minneopa
1929	5/23	Ballgame: Belgrade - 12, Rush Lake - 11
	10/10	Rebuild Seppman Mill
1930 – 1931		Refreshment Stand #2 Built
1931	2/5	State accepts Seppman Mill to MSP, 1931
	4/19	Additional 4.5 acres added to MSP
		Minor restorations to MSP
1932		Brow of south hill purchased (Peter Maiers farm)
	9/22	A.A. Anderson's drawing of Indian Execution
	11/9	*History of Minneopa* by Thomas Hughes reprinted
1936		Remodel Ranger's home, WPA
	9/30	Mankato Rifle Club lease from Seppman
1937		Steps to bottom of lower Falls built by WPA
1939	9/6	Seppman lawsuit over lease to Mankato Rifle Club
1942	5/15	Palmer Walnut Grove
	5/16	Palmer Grove dedication plaque
1947	4/21	New airport in Seppman's field
1949	3/24	Turn-in parking lot on Hwy 68
	5/23	Blue Earth County 4-H Event, Sunday Observance
1954		Blue Earth County ditch #48 channelized
1955	6/21	Seppman Mill Roadside Parking Area project with sign
1957	1/30	Seppmann Mill restoration
1959		Roof and stone walls repaired and stucco removed from exterior of Seppman Mill
1967	4/21	Minneopa expansion
		Minneopa State Park Natural/Recreational Park ACT (Active Community Thought)
		Mankato Area Chamber of Commerce formed
		Picnic shelter built in upper Minneopa State Park
		Expansion east of Minneopa Creek
1968	6/28	Minneopa expansion completed
	9/30	New trail at Minneopa
	12/31	450 acre expansion at Minneopa State Park
1969		A new 125 foot fence, tunnel to creek
1971		Seppman Mill and Minneopa State Park entered in the National Register of Historic Places
1971-74		Seppman Mill Roadside Parking Area on Hwy 68 removed
1972		Memorial plaque for 35 acres east of creek, donations
		New shower and restroom built at campground
1973		Tree planting in Minneopa State Park
1975		Installation of water lines to new picnic area of campgrounds

1975		Upgrade road to Seppman Mill and parking lot
		Turn-off lane at Highway #68, at Park entrance
		Volunteer Park Naturalist
1976	6/10	Minneopa State Park Visitors Center opening
		Minneopa State Park management plan
1985		Williams donates land for Williams Nature Center; 1983-1985
1986	6/5	Minneopa Falls, $3.00 charge, Ken Berg
1992	5/18	Bird banding
	6/18	Minneopa State Park, Seppman Mill project
1993	8/14	Minnesota River Trail closed
1994	4/7	New trail (Minnesota River Loop) at Minneopa State Park
1997	6/11	Minneopa's water is cause for concern
1998	6/?	Friends of Minneopa State Park formed
1998		Statutory boundary expanded another 1,475 acres for a total of 2,687 acres - western area towards Judson along Minnesota River
		County Road 69 rebuilt, Minneopa Creek moved
1999-2000		New office building
1999		Snow Day cancelled - no snow!!
		Camper Cabin added to campground
2000		Plaque for Ulmen farm
	11/13	DM&E Railroad expansion would damage MSP
2001	4/21	New life for Minneopa shelter (Pavilion)
2003	8/14	Minneopa song written
2004	1/7	Lake Crystal Ethanol Plant to be built
	10/10	Community Enrichment - Meyering Center seed collection
	10/21	Reestablishing Prairie Savanna at Minneopa State Park
	10/24	Craig Beckman, Assistant Manager of Minneopa State Park
2005	4/20	Highway #69, sinkhole near Minneopa State Park
	5/14	Centennial - Minneopa State Park, Natural Wonders – geology, waterfalls, flowers and birds
	6/5	Centennial Open House - birds, waterfalls and Seppman Mill
	7/3	Centennial - Minneopa memories, old fashioned picnic, band, cake, rootbeer, games
	10/?	Start Handicapped Trail renovation to the Falls
	10/?	Community Enrichment, Meyering Center, Seed Collection
2006		Geocaching allowed at Minneopa State Park
		Handicapped Trail completed to the Falls

Township 108 North.

Range XXVII West.

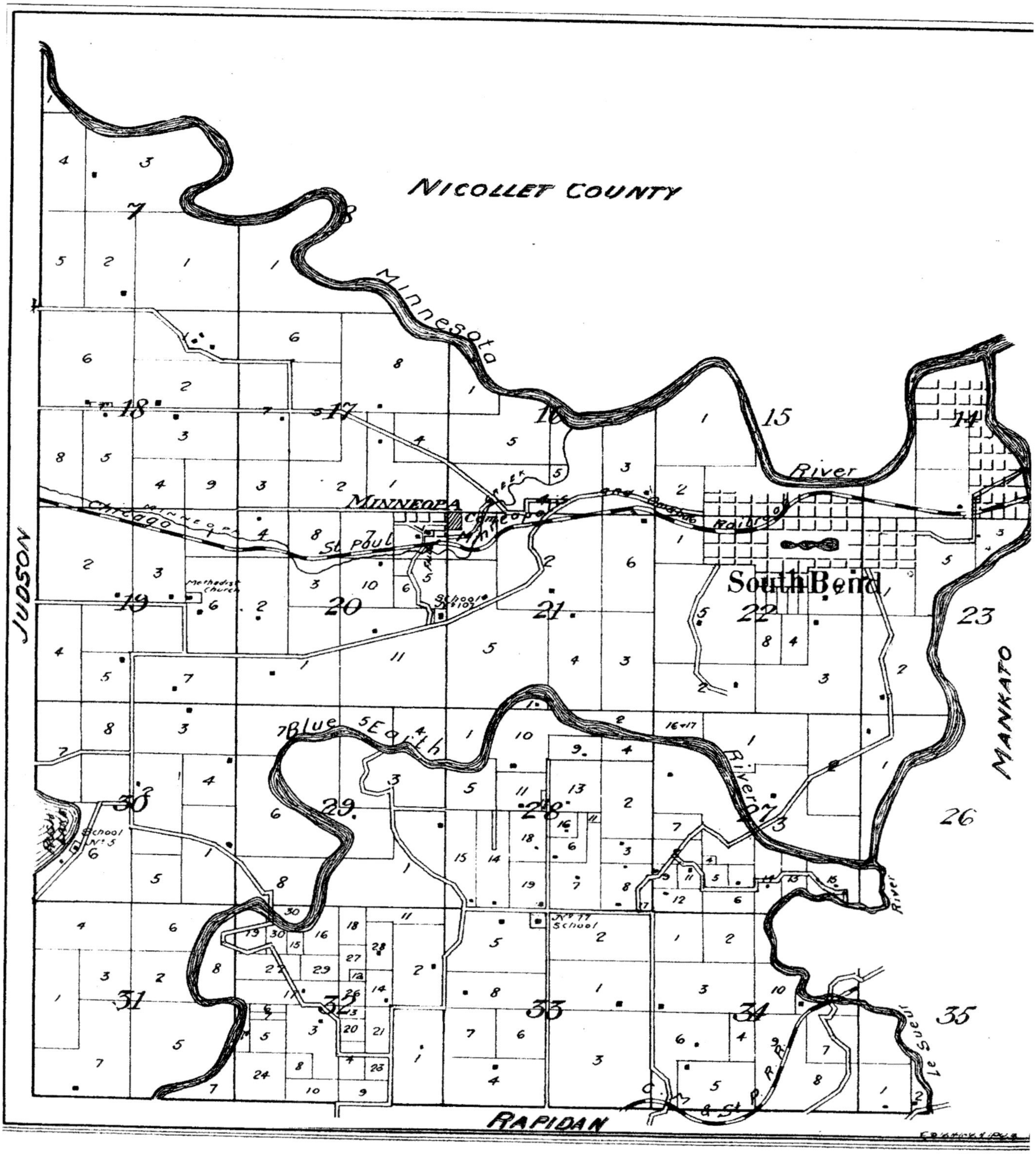

NICOLLET COUNTY

Minnesota

JUDSON

Chicago

Minneopa

St Paul

MINNEOPA

Methodist Church

School No 102

SouthBend

River

MANKATO

Blue Earth

River

School No 5

School No 77 School

Rapidan

RAPIDAN

Le Sueur River

C. & St. P. R. R.

1   4   3   7   8
5   2   1
6   8
2   18   17   10   15   14
3   4   5
8   5   4   9   3   2   1
2   3   19   20   21   22   23
6   2   10   6   8   4
4   5   11   5   9   3   8   4
5   7   1   3   2
8   3   7   8   1   10   9   4   13   26
7   2   5   11   13   2
30   29   28   16   12
6   3   5   18   16   12
1   15   14   19   7   8   17
4   6   30   16   18   11   2   1   3   10   35
19   30   15   27   28   5
3   2   8   27   29   13   2   31   32   26   14   33   34
1   20   21   7   6   6   4
5   23   1   3   5   8
7   24   8   10   9   4   7

105

Early plat map for the town of South Bend

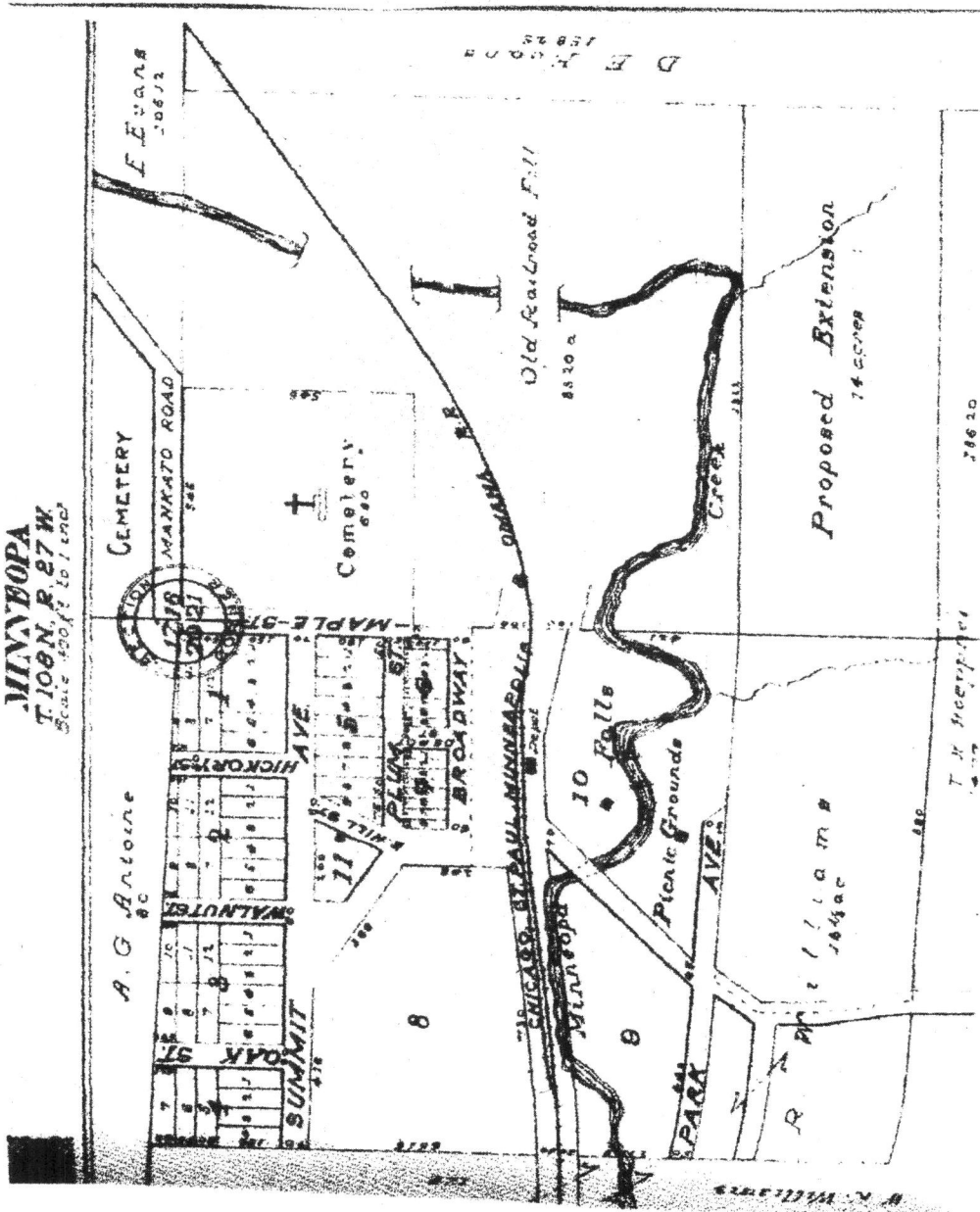

Early plat map for the town of Minneopa

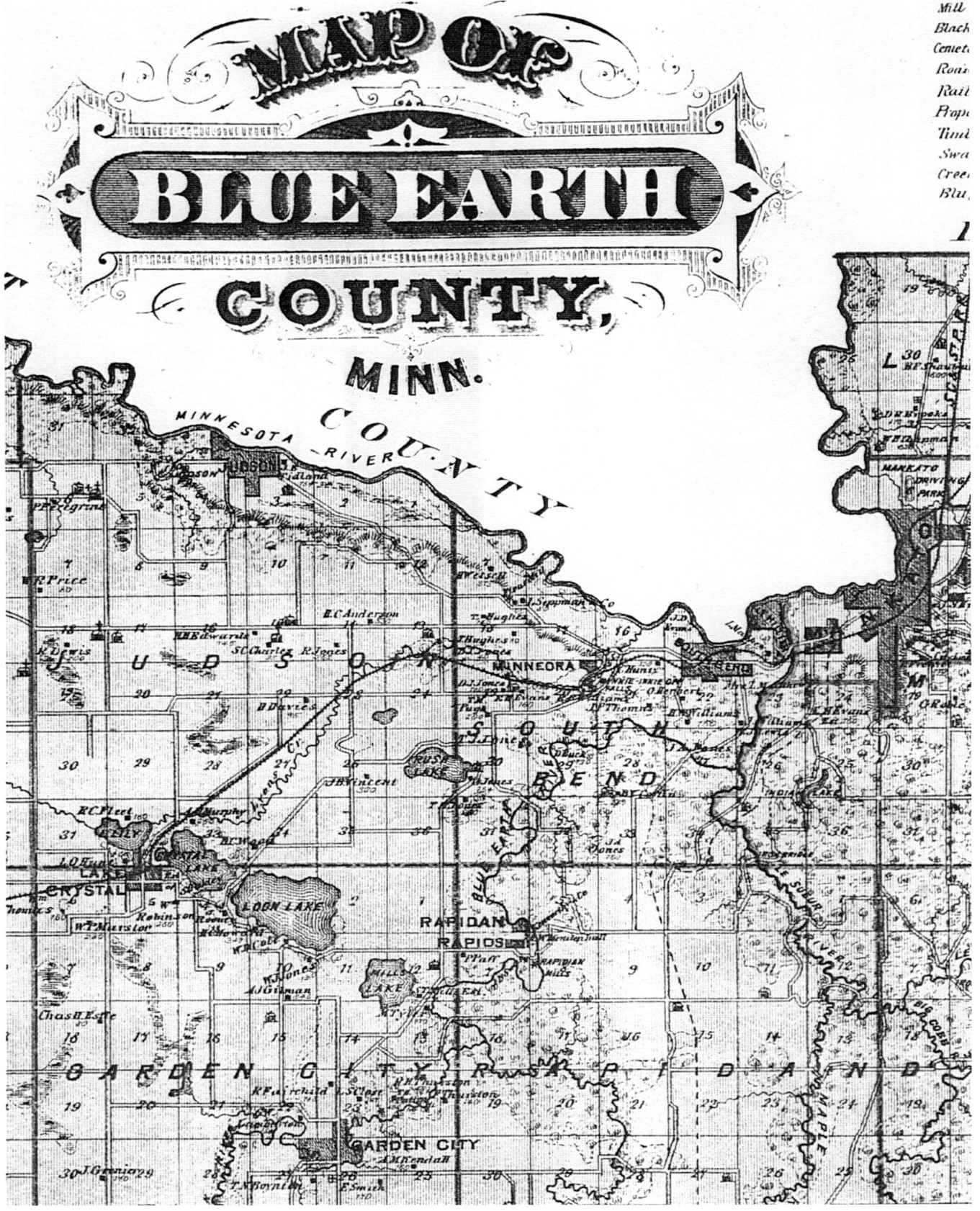

Partial map of Blue Earth County showing towns of Minneopa and South Bend *1874*

Aerial view of Minneopa State Park with current Park boundaries highlighted (MN State Parks map)

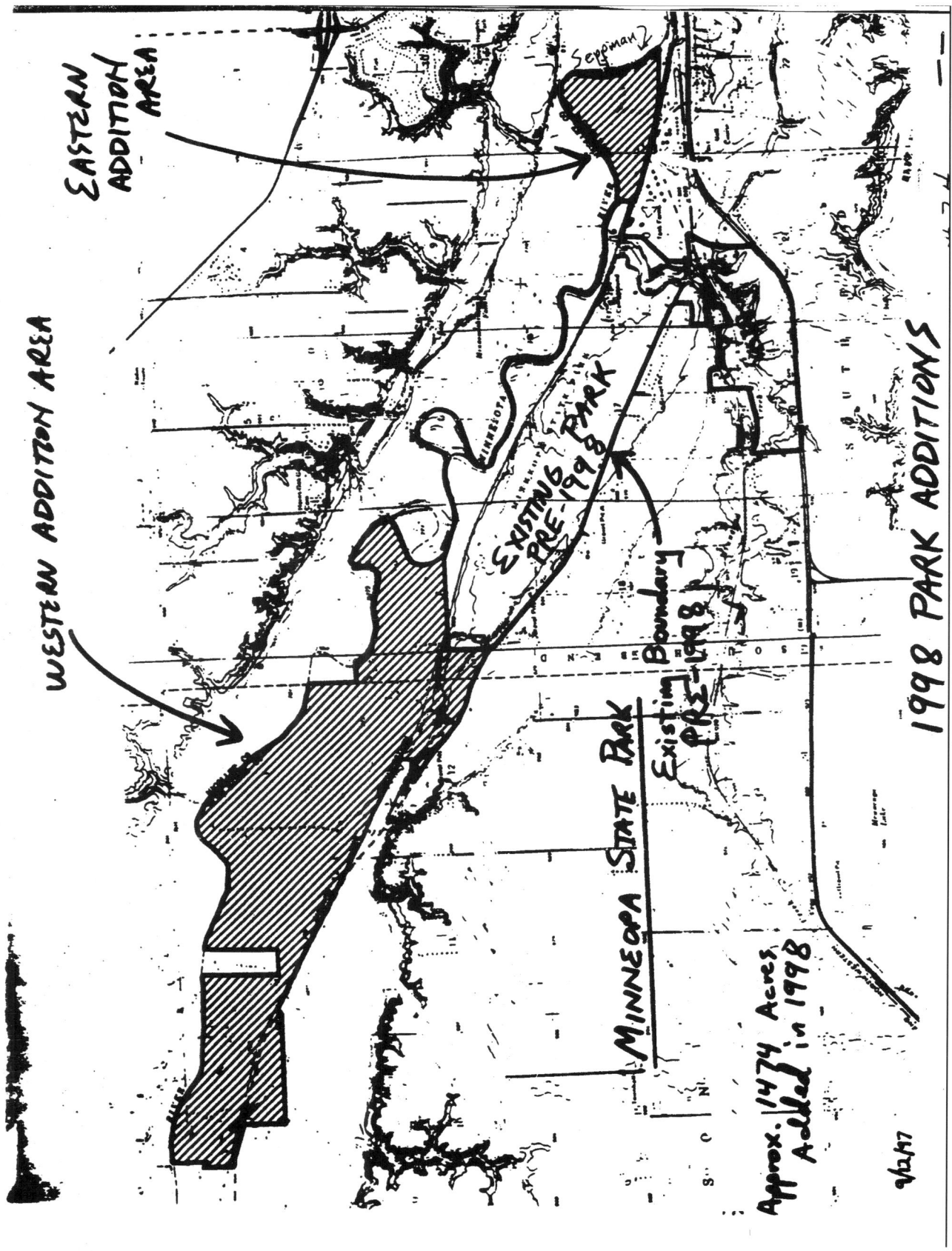

(MN State Parks map)

Public use map of Minneopa State Park *2007 (MN State Parks map)*

MINNEOPA STATE PARK

See This Area of Park Enlarged Below

Minnesota River

Minneopa Creek

Statutory park boundary

MANKATO, 3 miles

Respect Private Property
Ask First

Because lands exist within the boundaries of this park that are not under the jurisdiction of the D.N.R., check with the park manager if you plan to use facilities such as trails and roads other than those shown.

68
169
60
90
129
69
117

0.3 k
0.3 k
0.4 k
0.5 k
1.9 k
1.6 k
0.9 k

JUDSON, 7 miles

Seppman Windmill

Minneopa Creek

South Route Bike Trail

Note: Trail loop around falls is closed to skiers.

Statutory park boundary

GARDEN CITY, 9 miles
LAKE CRYSTAL, 6 miles

TRAILS
..... Hiking/Skiing
+++++ Hiking Club Trail/Ski
— — Biking
S Directional arrows apply to winter ski trails only.
All ski trails are rated easy.
1.0 k Trail distances are shown in kilometers

NORTH

0 1 2 3 4 5 Miles
0 1 2 3 4 5 Kilometers

FACILITIES
? Information
Park Office
Campground
Picnic Area
Historic Site
Overlook
Waterfall
Primitive Group Camp
Private Property
Public Use Prohibited (except on designated trails)

Acknowledgements

Craig Beckman

Elaine Feikema

Brand Frentz

Shelli Harrison

Neil Nurre

Carol Oney

Zachary Pelz

Jessica Potter

Steve Rose

Scott Salsbury

Daardi Sizemore

Gary Teipel

Howard Ward

Friends of Minneopa State Park

Back cover photo: **Minneopa prairie toward Seppman Mill** 2007 (G. Herbst photo)